# Lessons From The Garden

## Seeds of Wisdom for Parents

**PAMALA J. VINCENT**

## WHY I WROTE THIS BOOK

Parenting at its best is TOUGH. We worry constantly. Are we doing it right? Too much? Not enough? If we have great parents, we want to be just like them. If we were not blessed with great parents, we want to be better. I've often lamented that children should arrive with an instruction booklet, and options for mechanical breakdowns. I'd like to be able to call a service department, explain my problem and have a technician tell me how to fix it!

I was blessed with an older mentor—a woman who spoke my gardening language. The garden was and today remains the place I go to think, reflect, lick my emotional wounds, rebuild my resolve and rest. It was here my mentor, Rosie, began teaching me the ups and downs of gardening with parallel meanings for my parenting skills.

Her methods were subtle but rang true in my heart. When Rosie was promoted to Heaven, my continued growth in the garden grew me spiritually, emotionally, as a mother and wife as well as a woman. These stories are inspirational parables given to me while on my knees in the flowerbeds and dirt under my nails. It is my hope that you find seeds of wisdom that you can use in your garden and with your precious children.

~ Pamala J Vincent

Copyright © 2018 Pamala J. Vincent.
All rights reserved. No part of this book may be reproduced
or utilized in any form or by any means, electronic or mechanical,
including photocopying, recording, or by information storage
and retrieval system, without written permission from the author.

Produced by BookCreate
Seattle, Washington USA

ISBN 978-978-1-64440-955-8

Printed in USA

## A product of TREC

*THE LORD WILL GUIDE YOU ALWAYS;*
*HE WILL SATISFY YOUR NEEDS IN A SUN SCORCHED LAND*
*AND WILL STRENGTHEN YOUR FRAME.*
*YOU WILL BE LIKE A WELL-WATERED GARDEN,*
*LIKE A SPRING WHOSE WATERS NEVER FAIL.*

*ISAIAH 58:11*

## ~ DEDICATION ~

*Dreamers need to dream, but along the way they need inspiration, first-readers, editors, content fodder, and cheerleaders. It is impossible to list all who have contributed to my writing dream.*

*These stories started with a lady named Rosie, the first rose of summer, and her husband who convinced me to write for our local paper. That was ten years ago and 150 stories later, they're gathered in these volumes.*

*Thank you:*

*Antoinette Ellis, who taught me how to put on paper the words which have been loaned to me from heaven. And often reminding me, this gift was not for me, but was my responsibility to develop for others.*

*My daughter, Mother, Aunt, critique team and BoP, for always being available to edit and let me run ideas past them.*

*My husband, who continued to say, "Keep writing, I think you're on to something."*

*My father-in-law, who told me to be on the dock when my ship comes in.*

*My son for creating the graphic art and patiently walking me through how the 'pros' do it.*

*Thank you seems so little to give back for all that they have given; but Thank You.*

*Thank you all, for allowing my writing dreams to become a reality.*

## ~ CONTENTS ~

| | | |
|---|---|---|
| 1) | The First Rose of Summer | 9 |
| 2) | Flight Training | 17 |
| 3) | Butterfly Fight | 23 |
| 4) | Chasing Stillness | 29 |
| 5) | Slugs! | 35 |
| 6) | Master Gardener | 39 |
| 7) | Come Closer In | 43 |
| 8) | Grafting Growth | 49 |
| 9) | Anticipation! | 53 |
| 10) | Among the Roses | 59 |
| 11) | Mother's Ageless Wisdom | 67 |
| 12) | Chime Song! | 73 |
| 13) | A Good Run | 79 |
| 14) | Empty Nest | 85 |
| 15) | The Pono Way | 91 |
| 16) | Weed Guard | 101 |
| 17) | Never Under-Estimate | 105 |
| 18) | Passing on the Blessing | 111 |
| 19) | Fearful or Fearless Parenting? | 117 |
| 20) | Irritation or Inspiration? | 123 |
| 21) | The Heart of a Mother | 129 |
| 22) | I think I saw God today… | 135 |
| 23) | Wild Growth or Fruit Bearing | 141 |
| 24) | One More Lesson Before You Go | 145 |

# CHAPTER ONE

## THE FIRST ROSE OF SUMMER

*The aroma of a life shared that touches another's life may be the catalyst needed to stimulate vibrancy in their existence.*
~ Pamala J. Vincent

Every year, I await the arrival of our roses to announce the end of spring, and the coming celebration of summer. Their beauty is extraordinary and well worth waiting for, like some lives that cross our paths—short lived but vibrant. They leave me wishing I could capture their beauty forever. The moment they're gone, I begin to look forward to next year's bouquet.

My flowers grow much like people, interpreting God's sunlight into the handiwork of a multitude of colors. But in my entire garden there is nothing like the first rose of summer. My roses return every year to decorate the garden with their timeless classic fashion review and to leave their fragrance on the hands lucky enough to pick one while witnessing their revelry.

It is in the garden of my life that I met my flesh and blood rose of summer and the fragrance of this grand lady has not only enriched my life but her aromatic essence lingers on.

Rosie, was her name, called that by her dad. Born in March, he explained to her she was his precious "first rose of summer." I met Rosie after her stroke in 1979, when she was not expected to live much more than six months, requiring constant care. I was told she had been an active, vibrant gardener in her past, but the day's tasks at hand now included the difficult jobs of dressing and walking.

At 62, the stroke left her weak on one side and memory-challenged. Days would go by when she could not remember what she ate or the days of the week but could tell me childhood memories in such explicit detail, I was left dreaming of an era gone by. She often would forget my name, but never failed to identify every flower in my garden. Sitting for hours in my garden, she would watch and correct my planting techniques.

Rosie had a way of stating simple obvious facts. On good days when I was mature enough to not be irritated at her advice, I found great wisdom and comfort in her words. I would fight a battle of endless unwanted blackberry vines, only to hear her tell me, "Just keep pulling the annoying things out; they'll give up after a while." I smiled, wondering if she meant my own bad habits, grooming my new babies, or tending my young flower garden.

As our children grew, and my garden began to mature, Rosie encouraged me to plant flowers that would return every year, annually reducing my labors. This was my introduction to perennials, and lasting character traits for my children. "Invest in them today, and reap the benefits tomorrow," I could hear her say.

Rosie's favorite activity was to walk the property twice a day with either her little dog or my huge bear-sized black Lab. It was then that she met her toughest challenges, her battle with the dandelions! Most days she won the skirmishes by plucking the culprits from their soldier stances in the yard; other days bending over caused her to fall, where she would lie unable to get up until one of us found her lying in the grass along the trail. Each time we would frantically search for her, she cheerfully greeted us, "I knew you would come for me." She was never bitter about the wait; she was content to look around or take a nap.

Once when dusk had fallen and I could not find her in the dark, I called the paramedics. After they formed a search party, knowing the route she usually took through the woods to the creek, we fanned out. Before long the spotlight fell upon her lying on her side just off the path. As I prayed, "Dear Lord, let her be alive," she called my name and said, "I knew you would find me and come pick me up!" Her trust in me grew a lump in my throat that brought tears to my eyes. Just as I was chastising myself for not paying closer attention to the time when she left, she surprised us all by trying to get me a date with several good-looking firemen and paramedics! Thinking she was delusional, they looked at me with concerned-filled voices asking, "Is she ok?" I laughed through my embarrassment and nodded my head, "Yes, she's fine! This is her idea of being funny!"

As my garden plot and children grew, Rosie made suggestions for plants that brought great beauty and color among their established friends. She cautioned me not to over-plant, to learn to see what it would look like in a few years and to be patient. Over planting, over committing the space God has given me to grow and bloom in, has always been a struggle for me. Remembering her advice, I try to be patient waiting for God's work to be accomplished in His time frame, not mine.

She had the uncanny ability to compliment me on my parenting and remind me that she loved me, just at the moments I needed it most. As the demands of motherhood and life in general pressed in upon me, I found solace in my garden talking with Rosie. Life slowed to a more manageable pace there and I could make a corner of my world more beautiful, with dirt under my nails, and walk away with a sense of accomplishment.

We planted pink geraniums and roses to offset the blue flowers that lined the front flowerbed. As summer manifested itself in full color, I worked hard to keep the weeds and dandelions plucked so that Rosie wouldn't attempt to pick them and tumble over.

Early one summer, she developed a lump on her throat that began to grow. The diagnosis was terminal cancer allowing her only six weeks to live. She never understood the diagnosis, and we all lived with the knowledge this rare, one of a kind beauty would be tending eternal gardens with angels very soon. As her weakening body kept her from her daily walks, she was able only to make it to my garden. I was careful to take time to stop my busy life and discover the wealth of her memories, storing every word in my heart; her favorite song ('In the Garden'), her favorite dress, and foods. I felt like I was cramming for a final exam and had to retain the answers for my sake and her legacy.

She felt strongly that when she died, she was to be cremated; her husband was not to spend money fussing over her. "If anyone wants to send flowers, they should do it while I am alive, not after," she was often quoted as saying. As the closing of summer approached, so did her life. I remember her last day was a clear, crisp, fall day. Knowing something was wrong, as she struggled to breathe, she wanted her husband and me near. When she labored to speak and I asked her what she wanted, she simply said, "Talk." I questioned her, "You? Me?" and she pointed to me. I have always been one that can keep up a steady flow of chatter, but somehow idle words seemed so undignified for this grand rose who lay withering.

I sang her favorite songs and quoted Bible verses she knew. Knowing her love for the outdoors, I talked about the colors of the fall leaves, the sound of them crunching under my feet, the feel of the sun on my face and the crisp, cool breeze on my arms. She smiled a weak smile, watching me as I continued describing the smell of autumn leaves that the neighbors were burning. I brought in my Lab, and he very gently stuck his head between her hospice bed bars to nudge her hand. Smiling, she fought for every breath as she struggled to speak. I smoothed her hair from her brow encouraging her to rest, instead. She drifted off to sleep.

A few hours later, her husband summoned me back to their

house; she was asking for me. My black Lab, her walking partner and my constant companion, followed me to her porch with a worried look on his face while holding a leaf in his mouth like a gift. I hesitated as I began to climb the two small steps to the door of her house. I prayed God would give me the strength to finish the gift of our now eighteen-year old friendship. I yearned to be as strong as she had been in fighting her cancer. I wanted to see her all the way to the end of her earthly garden path. I had to muster the courage and fortitude to allow this blossom to fade from my life.

I entered the front door and proceeded to her bedside. Recognizing my voice, she smiled in her weakened state, making it clear that her husband and I were welcomed visitors as she prepared to embark on a journey we could not follow her on. It soon became apparent the breaths we were watching were her last.

Struggling as we said our good-byes, assuring her we were fine, we gave her permission to go on without us. She took one last breath.

Before today, I remembered fearing death: but, as I held her in my arms, and looked into her face, I watched her cross over from this life to a peaceful world beyond. Her departure into heaven was quiet and dignified. There was no stopping the grief I felt for myself and her dear husband. But the aroma Rosie left behind in the garden of my heart is there to stay.

Time has passed and every spring brings a strong reminder that soon the roses will bloom again. Rosie's ashes will rest as a perennial in the garden she loved to visit.

One year following Rosie's death, I began to write down the lessons she had taught to me during our special gardening times. As a rookie mom, eager to do my very best raising our children, I remember thinking I was so blessed to have this kind of wisdom at my fingertips. I began to practice daily all of Rosie's lessons, until one day when I was elbow deep in the dirt, Christ began to demonstrate to me my own seeds of wisdom. I learned timing, weeding, patience and sowing both in the garden and with our children. Although our children are now grown, the seeds that were planted inspired me to parent at my best. I pray you find your own *Seeds of Wisdom* amid the following stories.

• • •

**Parent Prayer:** Thank You, Lord, for turning loss into gain for my family: for teaching us to value life and the advice of those who have gone before us.

**Seeds of Wisdom:** Every parent needs a quiet place to sit, think and unwind; but also a place where intimate conversations with your child may happen. Build a garden!

**Gardening Tip:** Place many resting places within the garden, along with meandering paths.

# CHAPTER TWO

# FLIGHT TRAINING

1 Thessalonians 2:11-12 (NIV)
"For you know that we dealt with each of you as a father deals with his own children, encouraging, comforting and urging you to live lives worthy of God, who calls you into his kingdom and glory."

Chester, a down covered Canada gosling was given to me shortly after he'd been rescued. He spent hours with me as I weeded and watered the garden. Chester and I became a quick study of each other's grunts and coos. And like I had done with my children, I began to interpret what each one of his sounds meant. When we would lose sight of each other, he honked as if to holler, "Mom? Where are you?" and I'd answer him, "I'm over here," and he'd run to me.

Each day Chester would follow me on the trail through the woods as I took my morning walk. My neighbor would wave to me and call out, "Well, well, there goes Mother Goose."

The question was asked by many, "When will the goose fly?" As a concerned surrogate mother, I began to worry that his wings would not develop strong enough to carry his increasing body weight. The next morning as we began our daily walk, I slowly increased my pace. Chester stretched out his wings and ran behind me. Increasing to a jog, my heart almost broke when running as fast as he could he called out, "Gook, goooook," as if to say, "Wait, mom, why are you doing this?" I continued to jog just out of his reach, until he finally extended his wings and took his first flight.

I was so excited, I almost fell into a blackberry bush cheering and applauding him! Just to let me know it was his idea and not mine, he flew over just low enough to give me a good thunk on the back of the head with one of his wings

Chester's flying was the beginning of his arrival into young adulthood. Like most teens announcing their arrival, he became belligerent and obstinate. Thinking the world revolved around him, he began to let me know he thought his schedule was the most important, and that it was an honor when he allowed me to be with him.

He no longer cooed at me, but hollered as if he was angry with me. Loving him as only a mother could, I allowed him his annoying efforts toward independence, but worried no one would survive his "coming of age."

Although I hadn't felt he was ready to be independent, at the urging of family, I reluctantly agreed to set him free into the wilderness. We drove to a near-by pond where we knew Canada Geese habitually gather. Willingly, he got out of the truck to go swimming. Once in the water he attempted to socialize with the other geese, only to be run off by males that were guarding females on nests near the pond. Chester returned to me. Convinced my presence was impeding his adjustment to being free, we climbed into the truck to leave.

As we turned onto the highway, I heard a familiar "gook, gooook!" It was Chester with his "wait for me" honk. Looking out the window, I could see him following the truck high in the sky. Untrained for this, his wings were not strong enough to sustain the six-mile flight home. Needing rest, he landed in the middle of the highway and called to me.

I yelled at my husband, "Stop! He's going to get hit!" As we pulled to the side of the road, I leaped out and desperately called to him. We made eye contact and just as he took to the air, he was hit broadside by a car.

The next scene looked like a feather bed exploding. I dropped to my knees sobbing, "I killed him! He trusted me, and I killed him!"

My husband ran to him and returned sadly asking, "What do you want to do with him?" Chester was still alive but bleeding profusely from a chest wound and his leg was broken in several places. In my arms, Chester laid his head on my chest, his quiet noises mixing with my sobs.

As we reached home, Chester went into serious shock. Knowing the end was near, I called the vet, and was told there wasn't anything more that could be done for him and I should consider putting him out of his misery. The tears ran down my cheeks and I apologized to him over and over. I sat in his pen for two days attempting to nurse him back to health.

There is a happy ending. Chester pulled through and, although he walks with a limp these ten years later, he still rules the yard!

Through my goose experiences, I learned a valuable lesson. In a world that moves our children from infants to adulthood in record time, I learned to trust my instincts. I no longer allow others who don't spend as much time with my children to dictate what and when is best for them.

Today's children are making decisions that have potentially life-threatening consequences before they've even learned to manage their acne.

Life readiness arrives on individual perfectly timed body clock that gets out of sync when it's are sped up or slowed down. As the "flight-trainer," one of my many parenting jobs is to determine when my children are ready for flight. You, too, must become a flight trainer who knows when the time is right to set your children's wings to flight.

• • •

**Parent Prayer:** Lord, teach me to seek You in all things while raising Your children. Rein me in when I might push too fast or too hard, and poke me when I need to allow them to grow when I'm not ready to let go.

**Seeds of Wisdom:** No one knows your child's readiness better than you do. Avoid listening to too many opinions that do not have your knowledge of your child.

**Garden Tip:** Goose-raising is best left for the birds to accomplish. Chester is now twenty-four years old and as independent as he was the day we attempted to set him free.

# CHAPTER THREE

# BUTTERFLY FIGHT

Jeremiah 29:11 (NIV)

"For I know the plans I have for you," declares the LORD,

"plans to prosper you and not to harm you,

plans to give you hope and a future."

"Momma, help!" cried my frantic four-year-old. Stubby little fingers tightly grasped a long twig: hanging mid-way down the branch was a chrysalis. The transparent covering was split and just barely visible were the bright velvet colors of a Viceroy butterfly's wings. It was easy to see why my son was so distraught; the butterfly appeared to be stuck . . . half in and half out. His movements demonstrated two distinct attributes for one so small: fight and perseverance.

I tried to calm my son's fears and explained that his treasured find would not die and that we could not help; it had to use its own power. The struggles were agonizing to watch. We held our breath, praying this tiny insect would become all that its maker intended.

Caterpillars, like our children, begin life dependent. Once they move from early life to adolescence, they take on an entirely new look. At about this new stage, the butterfly's wings grow three to five times the length of its own body. The excruciating squeeze through the tiny opening in the cocoon is precisely the action needed to move the gel-like fluid from the torso to the tips of the wings. The great effort it takes to break free is, in fact, the process that fills the wings of the young adult for successful aviation. Without this challenge, the butterfly would be doomed to remain flightless.

Although it remained painful to watch the great struggles, my son began to clap for the butterfly each time minor progress was accomplished. He cheered and coaxed when it appeared the butterfly might give up the fight.

My desire is for my children to become like beautiful butterflies and learn to fly strong. But too often today, children are denied the right to struggle. Because we love our charges and want the best for them, we often interfere or lessen the blows of struggling, thinking we will make life easier for them.

As difficult as it is to watch, struggles are necessary to produce the perseverance and confidence needed in life to be accomplished adults. I'm learning to see that perseverance is the end product of uncomfortably stretching our wings. If I keep my children from difficulties as they grow, I rob them of their ability to soar and potentially curtail their independence. My role instead is to clap when they succeed, and to cheer when they look too tired to fight.

Parenting is one of the greatest responsibilities God will ever give us; the greatest blessings also, but the hardest work we've ever experienced. Our children have worn out our knees in prayer for them and yet have given us a history with the Father like none other.

I often, in my prayers, visually bring each one of my children by the hand to the feet of the Father and ask Him, "How shall I help them become all You designed them to be? Show me when to cheer, when to watch, and when to stay out of Your way. Thank You Lord that You love them more than I could ever understand or be capable of. Help them to be only satisfied by You, that all else pales in their lives without You."

My son and I held our breath as the butterfly finally squeezed itself completely out of what once was its protective capsule. We were awed as the rookie aviator stretched its fully functioning wings. And, as if to say good bye, turned away from us and took flight.

I marveled at such tenacity as the butterfly flew towards the bright colored flowers and never looked back. As a tear slowly slid down my cheek, I hugged my son closer to me. I could glimpse our future in the butterfly's departure. My ever-aware-blonde-headed-insect-lover saw my tear and patted my face with his chubby little hands, and said, "It's O.K., Mommy; he flies good."

**Parent Prayer:** Lord, help me to know when to restrain Our precious children and when to push, when to help and when to stand and watch. Lord, hold my hands when they must struggle in order to gain their wings.

**Seeds of Wisdom:** Be careful to allow your children to struggle, it teaches internal strength and tenacity. Overcoming obstacles empowers young people to triumph as adults.

**Garden Tip:** There are several types of flowers and bushes that attract butterflies to the garden. My favorites are the purple Butterfly Bush and the giant Sunflowers.

# CHAPTER FOUR

# CHASING STILLNESS

Psalms 46:10 (NIV)

"Be still and know that I am God."

I had one of those nights again last night. We were awakened by our goose, Chester, yelling for us to come help him because he was under attack. The two juvenile raccoons that live in our woods were out at three a.m. looking for an easy meal.

These are the bravest (or dumbest) raccoons I've ever met. Earlier in the evening they had come to the sliding glass door, stood on their hind legs, placed their little hands on the window and pressed their noses against the glass. They stood there staring at me, while I watched TV, as if to say, "Hey, lady, did you know the cat's food dish is empty?" In an attempt to keep them away from the house, I opened the door and yelled at them to go home.

They took a few steps back, but then sat down, hands clasped, and looked at me from behind their masks, perplexed, as if I hadn't understood their request. After repeating this scenario several times, they finally left.

Later when I was curled up in bed with the window open, I heard Chester who knows he can yell for us and we'll come running. In fact, he yells so often, my husband has begun to call him our twenty-pound rooster. Chester hollers when the sun comes up, when the city bus goes by and when the trucker who still uses his Jake-brakes comes down the hill past our house. But tonight's squawk held a tone of serious urgency. When my husband turned the big spotlight on the pen, we could see Chester standing in the middle of his cage staring towards the house as if to say, "Hurry UP!" Beside the enclosure were two sets of eyes staring back at us, like two kids caught with their hands in the cookie jar. My husband yelled at them to go home, but they just stood there blinking their eyes in the light. He eventually had to walk out there with a stick and bang on the pen to convince the raccoons to retreat into the woods. We then went back to sleep, until 5 a.m. when Chester announced the city bus driving by the house.

The morning light, as it often does, beckoned us to get up and share the day. We pulled on our warm sweats, and coffee cups in hand, walked the trail to the creek looking for our juvenile delinquents. We knew it was a long shot, but we were hoping to find their home and maybe encourage them to move farther into the woods or downstream. Luckless in our search, we started back up the trail towards home watching the dog run ahead of us with her nose in the air signaling something was near.

If a person glanced quickly, it would appear as if the woods were empty today, but knowing what we knew from the night's escapades, we stopped and just stood there listening and observing. We became the spectators rather than the hunters, and we were rewarded for our efforts. Way up high, about fifty feet up in the fork of the old cedar tree, sat a masked bandit silently watching us. When he saw us see him, he ducked down lower but never took his eyes off of us. His buddy wasn't as brave and headed up the side of the tree putting another forty feet between us.

I had to smile as I realized their 'operation look-out' was built strategically so that they could see the garden, our back porch and the goose pen. That means they knew exactly when I fed the goose, the cat, and filled the squirrel and bird feeders! Our delinquents were actually quite clever! They had learned the rewards of strategic stillness.

In our past attempts to track them down aggressively, chasing them in the dark through the woods, we were rewarded only when we had given up and stood silently. As if the forest needed to reinforce the lesson we were learning about stillness, while we stood there quietly, a mother doe and yearling appeared on the trail where we had just been walking. The doe, already aware of us and keeping a safe distance while she ushered her young one towards the thicket, quietly let us know that if we did not move quickly she would allow the privilege of this morning's meeting. The yearling, on the other hand, was more curious than cautious and wandered closer towards us until mom cut him off and with a flick of her tail insisted he follow her.

Our dog stood reluctantly silent beside us watched by two masked bandits, a curious fawn and a cautious doe. The young rabbits sat on the edge of the trail watching to see how soon they would have to dart into the tall grass to avoid the dog and a beautiful song wafted down from a fir tree on the other side of the trail. What a magical morning, like a Discovery channel episode, but better—because we stood in the midst of the magic.

It's going to be tough to fill the birdfeeder without being reminded that I'm being observed. Every day when I walk the trail through the woods, I've felt as if I was being watched, and today, I know my instincts were right. I often walk to work off the tension that gets wound up in me during the day, to somewhat synthetically produce an inner calm. But, today the lesson the woods taught me is that I must stop chasing stillness. And that if I expect to be rewarded, I must simply be still. I can only imagine how many times the birds, the rabbits, the doe and the bandits have watched me power-walk along the trail, maybe they even shook their heads, wondering how long it will take me to get it.

• • •

**Parent Prayer:** Teach me, Lord, to slow down, to spend more time with You. Train me to hear Your quiet whispers and grant me the ability to pass on that kind of listening to Our children. Remind me, Lord, that while I need exercise to calm and center myself, I also need to simply be still.

**Seeds of Wisdom:** When children are young, we do them a great service to teach them how to be quiet and still—alone with themselves. When times in their lives grow difficult, this practice of being calm will help them to have time to make better choices.

**Garden Tip:** Feed and fill feeders early in the day and limit the amount you give your outdoor pets. This will avoid unwanted nighttime guests.

## CHAPTER FIVE

# SLUGS!

Proverbs 18:10 (NIV)
"The name of the LORD is a fortified tower;
the righteous run to it and are safe."

"Someday when I get to heaven, I'm going to ask God about slugs!"

Slugs are the gardener's plague in areas where the environment is moist. Simply, they are snails (gastropods) without shells and their slimy bodies can destroy a garden quicker and more completely than any other predator. A slug's weapon is a rough, tongue-like organ with tiny tooth-like 'dentils' used for munching your prize flowers and vegetables to satisfy their ferocious appetite. They have the ability to self-procreate by the hundreds every thirty days and can smell fresh plants from a very great distance. No garden is safe from these predators unless a gardener faithfully protects each plant.

I spend countless hours in my garden, praying for individuals that I know, needs that I've heard, and today again my conversation with God had been interrupted by slugs. I often contemplate the how's and why's of God's universe, and though I try to be open-minded, I cannot find one reason for Him to have created SLUGS! With dirt under my nails, and a liquid slug-bait bottle in my hand, I begin my ritual of tracing circles around every plant in the garden.

I try to make certain that each new plant receives the same meticulous care. First I work the soil, adding compost for growth, and then carefully draw a barrier of slug-bait poison around each young flower. Slugs can be disastrous to new and old plants alike; they can completely lay to waste an unprotected novice. Even the older well-established plants come away with battle scars from waging war against these ferocious enemies.

It was during a day of 'garden praying' that I heard my Master Gardener's voice. He reminded me slugs are like the sins in the garden of my life. Each time I learn a new lesson from God, I need to be as meticulous a caretaker of my life as I am of the flowers in my garden. If a new stem of growth is not carefully tended and guarded with a barrier of prayer, its truth can be stolen from me.

Slugs in my garden are only harmful if I am unprepared for them. Likewise, sin can rob from the saint if he is unprepared. I grow best when fertilized well by the Scriptures and have a barrier of prayer to guard my development and maturation.

**LESSONS FROM THE GARDEN:** *Seeds of Wisdom for Parents*

• • •

**Parent Prayer:** Lord, help me to be prepared for the predators of the world and to train Our children to recognize 'destroyers'. Teach me to build boundaries like the armor on a warrior so that I might not fall into the clutches of sinful choices but will stand strong because of You. Remind me, Lord, to run to You. Help me to be vigilant to pray boundaries around Our children until they can do it well for themselves.

**Seeds of Wisdom:** When children are young, establishing boundaries creates strong habits and security as they mature. We started saying things like: When you're sixteen and you start dating, or we're family, no matter what it is, we go through it together.

**Gardening Tips:** To win the war against destructive slugs you'll need a good offense; there are also natural means, such as:

- Placing a pan of beer or a yeast and water mixture near the garden. The slugs will be drawn to it, climb in and drown.

- You can also fill a closed coffee size can ¼ of the way with soapy water. Make a one inch hole half way up the can. Slugs will climb in, fall in and drown.

- Planting Marigolds close together outside the garden will draw the slugs away from your vegetables.

# CHAPTER SIX

# THE MASTER GARDENER

Psalms 139:14 (NIV)
"I praise you because I am fearfully and wonderfully made;
your works are wonderful, I know that well."

"Exquisite!" exclaimed my neighbor, a self-proclaimed amateur gardener. "Look at the shape and form of those trees." Each branch was painstakingly shaped to compliment itself individually and the tree as a whole. "It must take years to develop such an artful skill! Only an expert could create such a perfect symmetry."

We went eagerly to find the master gardener of the nursery to ask how we could do the same thing with our trees.

"First you must have a plant that chooses to grow towards the sun and is flexible," he said.

My neighbor and I carefully selected and purchased a 'flexible' healthy tree seedling and set out to develop a unique design of our own. I quickly lost interest in the slow process, but my neighbor continued to follow the master gardener's instructions. He trimmed, spaced, fertilized, and weighted his prodigy. Months went by, life grew difficult for my neighbor and the tree-shaping project was forgotten. The grass grew tall and blackberries soon took over the tree, nearly choking its ability to reach for the sun. Goats were borrowed to help control the weeds, but instead of just eating the weeds, they broke the tree in two and stripped it of its leaves.

Years passed but under the weight of weeds and blackberries, the tree still grew.

Life slowed a bit, and in an effort to recapture his yard, my neighbor again began to cut away the acre of weeds and overgrown grass. As he struggled with the blackberries, now woven to a tangled mass over six feet high, he remembered the little tree in which he had set so much hope. Slowly unwinding the thick vines and branches, the tree began to come into view. Wrestling with the last determined vine, my neighbor fell to the ground as he finally won the tug-of-war.

While sitting on the ground looking up at his prize, he saw the most uniquely shaped fruit tree. The twists and turns that beautified the branches were truly unique. Beyond the unequaled beauty of it all, the tree bore fruit—perfect, sweet, exquisite fruit. The amateur gardener sat amazed at how the little tree's tenacity and single-minded focus had fashioned its limbs. Reaching for the sun, the branches met each obstacle, altering the course only long enough to go around a barrier and then to resume the original path. The flexible seedling had proven itself to be determined, purposeful and steadfast enough to fulfill its potential, in spite of the obstacles thrown in its way. And it bore fruit.

Stepping back as an observer of such examples of life, like the little tree, I see how trials are opportunities to contour my growth and add that beauty to my character. Each of my experiences, more often the bad rather than the good, shapes and defines me. And when I remain steadfast in my pursuit of the **Son**, welcoming the hurdles, I too can become "Exquisite!"

• • •

**Parent Prayer:** Lord, remind me that You ultimately know all the twists and turns of my life and I will trust You for what my life is and will be. Help me to mentor Our children to understand that You make all things good for them, if they will bring obstacles in their lives to You.

**Seeds of Wisdom:** One of our many jobs as parents is to recognize the unique talents and personality traits of each of our children and direct them to or through them. Help them to see they are distinctive and should embrace it rather than attempting to fit in with others.

**Garden Tip:** Tying a weight on the end of a string attached to a flexible young tree and carefully trimming branches will change the direction of growth in a young tree, creating unique shapes.

# CHAPTER SEVEN

# COME CLOSER IN

Psalm 73:28 (NIV)

"But as for me, it is good to be near God. I have made
the Sovereign LORD my refuge; I will tell of all your deeds."

"Are the angels out yet?" I heard a small voice say.

Looking up from my weeding, I could see the twins standing just outside the garden gate, the world at their feet as five years old. The smaller of the girls, Kristen, was almost completely hidden behind her twin. Leslie is the bolder of the two. She's been here many times before and knows she doesn't need to stay outside the gate, but she waits for her sister to catch up. Their golden blonde curls, huge blue eyes and gentle sprinkling of freckles make them look like cherubs. They are identical twins in every way except for their personalities.

Leslie is interested in everything around her and approaches life with a 'what's next?—bring it on' attitude. Kristen often waits for Leslie before she will try anything, choosing always to be safe.

It was Leslie who first ventured beyond their property boundaries, running through the trails in the woods that border my garden. She asked me one day why I had built my garden. I shared with her that this is where I come when I need to think or if I have a problem and I need to pray. I told her about the times I spent in my grandmother's garden when I was a child and how I loved the smell of the old roses. I also shared with her my favorite stories of Thumbelina and The Secret Garden. In wide-eyed innocence, she asked if she could come and think in the garden, too. I often find her sitting under the arbor talking or singing to herself or to my cat.

One day while having lunch with a friend, we found several beautiful four-inch tall life-like plastic angels. I hung them up in the garden in places, that if you look carefully, you will find them. Leslie enjoys searching for the garden angels and today she had brought her sister to help her look for them.

Kristen, being timid, is not sure she wants to come inside the garden, so I try to assure her that it's fine to enter and search for the angels. Leslie whispers to me that Kristen is afraid.

Leslie bolts from flower-bed to flower-bed searching the places where she has found the angels in the past: inside the Lace Leaf Maple, under the Blue Cadet Hosta, sitting on a rose stalk, or next to the pond. Kristen stays put at the entrance even when Leslie finds an angel and calls to Kristen to come and see.

"I found one; it's the angel with the pink dress; come and see!" she calls out.

"I'll look from here," Kristen calls back to her sister, still holding tightly to the metal arch at the entrance. Standing tip-toe on the rock wall, Kristen struggles to see what Leslie is talking about.

"You won't really be able to see them well," Leslie answers back to her reluctant sibling, "unless you come closer in!"

"I'm afraid to see them," Kristen admits to her adventurous twin sister.

"But you're missing it . . . ; please, come closer in," Leslie does her best to get Kristen to move from her safe place.

I sit quietly watching and wondering if Kristen will leave her sentinel post at the garden gate and experience the garden angels.

This scenario reminds me of life and people in general. There really are two kinds of personalities: those who experience life with all the gusto of a wildfire and those who 'play it safe'.

I identify with both Leslie and Kristen's spirits. I use to be so shy that I was timid about everything. I was afraid of making a mistake and I was afraid I would not know what to do if a situation was difficult. I lacked confidence to try. I use to worry more about what others would think of me than what I thought of me. And I'm not sure where I got the idea that taking a risk is always a bad idea.

One summer, I discovered at a Vacation Bible School that I was specifically chosen and loved for who I am. I learned that I was promised an abundant life. With this information in hand, I decided to set my sails to the wind whether or not I knew how to sail the vessel perfectly. And to everyone's surprise, including my own, my boat not only floats but I'm becoming a good sailor.

I believe today, that life is for living to the absolute fullest I can experience. I've made mistakes, but as long as I learn from them they aren't really mistakes. I've risked and benefited from taking risks. I am no longer missing out. And I am no longer shy.

To remain overly-cautious, puts a person in danger of giving their power away—never experiencing life to its fullest. I chose instead to attempt to become all I can be.

Today, like Leslie, I am willing to risk, to try and fail, to move out of my comfort zone, and to attempt new endeavors. I'm ready to unwrap the gifts life is willing to give to me, and to turn my sails into the wind. I choose to live life as if I'm leaving it tomorrow. I am thankful I heard the promise in the voice of Christ that also said to me, "Come closer in!"

• • •

**Parent Prayer:** Lord, thank You that Your arms draw me close when I might be too afraid to step out into the world. I'm thankful You help me to live my life without regrets. Help me to show Our children that in this world, YOU are a dependable, safe place to draw near to.

**Seeds of Wisdom:** Help your children to set goals, take calculated risks and try new things in order to build their self-esteem and memory bucket.

**Gardening Tip:** Adding unique, non-plant items to your garden, encourages visitors to slow down, to look around and spend some valuable time resting within the garden. Also planting flowers or placing rocks serve to earmark special times shared together.

# CHAPTER EIGHT

# GRAFTING GROWTH!

Psalms 73:26 (NIV)

"My flesh and my heart may fail, but God is the strength of my heart and my portion forever."

"It might grow, but it will never produce anything worth keeping," declared the nurseryman. "You might as well burn it and be done with it!"

An individual who enjoys a challenge, I took the little tree home. Nurturing it for three years, I was never rewarded with a single bud that remotely resembled an apple blossom, much less an apple. I was afraid the nurseryman's prediction was right.

One fall, my neighbor watched as I prepared to dig it up. As an individual who enjoys experimenting and hates to see waste of any kind, he said, "Mind if I give it a try?" Trusting in his green thumb, I nodded and gave him permission to try his skills.

Experienced at fruit producing, he gently grafted a healthy branch onto the young sapling. He gently spliced the two branches, one inside the other, and wrapped them in cotton strips to bind them together. With the newly introduced and grafted branch inserted and bound within the life flow of the barren tree, we waited for spring to see what would happen.

Seasons later, a neighbor of mine dropped by to chat. Knowing if you stand to talk with me long enough you will be put to work, she readily joined me. Digging together in the dirt, we planted tulip bulbs. She began to share her heartaches. We dropped each bulb one-by-one into the holes. Each time she complained of her personal shortcomings, I tried my best to encourage her. While I listened, I searched for words of wisdom to comfort her.

After successfully planting 200 bulbs, she sat down and said to me, "Thank you for letting me share your garden. You never tell me to just get lost. You always welcome me, and seem to be able to see good things in me. Man! I wish I had it all together like you!"

I laughed, assuring her that I didn't have it all together, that the only difference between us was I was older and had survived a few more lessons from the "University of Hard Knocks."

Turning her around as I pointed to it, I said, "See that barren little tree?"

"I see the tree loaded with apples over there, but I don't see the barren one you're talking about," she said, puzzled.

LESSONS FROM THE GARDEN: *Seeds of Wisdom for Parents*

"EXACTLY," I smiled knowingly. "A few years ago, a strong branch was grafted onto the barren tree. All it took was a little time for the tiny tree to bare good fruit. You'll produce, too; be patient with yourself!"

• • •

**Parent Prayer:** Lord, help me to graft myself within Your heart, so that I may draw strength from You and produce fruit that benefits others. Help me then to demonstrate the abiding in You necessary for Our children to be solidly grafted to Your life-giving flow.

**Seeds of Wisdom:** Teach children to memorize Bible verses, quotes and poems that have the potential to help them out in times of trouble. My mother taught me, "If in doubt, don't." This is a simple philosophy but it saved me many times. My father made us memorize the poem: Thank God for dirty dishes, they have a tale to tell; while other folks go hungry, we're eating very well. With home and health and happiness, we shouldn't want to fuss, for by this stack of evidence, God is Very good to us.

**Gardening Tip:** When growing young fruit trees, prune back to two blooms per branch in order to allow the apples to develop fully. Too many apples on each branch will drain the tree's energy and divert the growth away from the fruit.

# CHAPTER NINE

# ANTICIPATION!

Psalms 62:5 (NIV)

"Find rest, O my soul, in God alone; my hope comes from him."

In *The House at Pooh Corner*, A. A. Milne wrote that for Winnie the Pooh, *"Although eating honey was a very good thing to do, there was a moment just before you began to eat it which was better than when you were, but he didn't know what it was called."*

Gently fingering the little spheres of hope, I wonder how many more I can give a home to before the winter frost beats me by freezing the ground. Tulips, daffodils, and irises---the hope of spring, the bugler that winter is over. The anticipation of their expected arrival is almost as exciting as the moment they stick their heads up out of the soil. I always buy and plant the mixed packages of bulbs, so I never know what I'm getting, until each tuber smiles its unique smile wearing its new clothes.

Christmas is like that for me; it always holds the same excited expectation. Will there be Christmas snow? Will the turkey turn out right? What special events will surround our times together? You'd think after all these years, I'd be immune to the anticipation of Christmas, but I'm not. I guess the little girl in me just won't grow up.

In raising our children, we often told them the Christmas story from the Bible. We talked about that precious night when even the animals bowed down to the baby Jesus in the manger, and that on Christmas Eve, at midnight, the cows and sheep still bow down in reverence. Every year, with great excitement, dressed in slippered feet, warm P.J.'s with hot cocoa in hand, we would pile into the car and drive out to the country to find a farmer's field that we knew had cows and sheep. Quietly pulling the car up so our headlights lit up the field, we held our breath in expectation of catching them kneeling down at midnight.

Every year we would arrive at the same field, only to find that we had missed it, the cattle and sheep were already kneeling down. In awe and frustration, our little ones would confirm that in fact the animals did bow down to Jesus, but that next year we would need to be earlier to catch them in the act. Our adventure continued for ten years until they decided that cattle and sheep bow down when it gets dark to bed down for the night. There is an innocent sweet moment that lies somewhere just between the hope and the reality. Now many years later, they're grown but I miss their anticipation of precious little things, because for a moment—just a moment, but a glorious moment—everyone held their breath in excited anticipation.

It seems to me, in our hurry-up world, where we can often be more strangers than friends, you may, like me, miss the childlike wonder of anticipation—the hope and power of expectations, dreams and believing. I wonder why as adults we let that fresh quality die? I don't believe we stop dreaming, anticipating or hoping. I do believe we let 'it' get buried under rules, sensible things and the trappings of life. I know each time I hold a newborn baby, I look into the face and hope for the future rises up. There is an excitement within me, an anticipation of things to come. And I surmise, perhaps that's why Jesus arrived as an infant, not a six-foot tall warrior.

My fingers tingle from the cold ground, while I plant the unmarked bulbs, in expectation of what the hillside will look like next spring. It's good to expect great things. It's great to anticipate the gifts of life that lie just beneath the wrappings.

"What are you expecting?" As this year comes to a close and the new one begins, I wonder what things are to come and I'm filled with a sweet sense of anticipation.

• • •

**Parent Prayer:** Lord, teach my soul to wait only on You—to anticipate life lived for You. In this world where I may be tempted to focus on success for Our children, remind me often that life without You doesn't mean anything and all the accolades will be hollow without You.

**Seeds of Wisdom:** Start early in your family to build traditions. It's wonderful when your grown children return home and want to repeat their childhood antics. We loved the countdown between Thanksgiving and Christmas. We hung a paper chain up with something special to do every day like: 1) Go look at Christmas lights, 2) Drink hot chocolate on the porch watching the stars, 3) Take a picture with Santa, etc. We planted bulbs in the church flowerbed when each of the children was baptized. Every year the bulbs bloomed, they served as a reminder of their commitment.

**Garden Tip:** For winter beauty, intersperse plants with interesting shapes and colors even when their leaves have been shed, such as: Dwarf Blueberry bush, Jacob's staff, Weeping Cherry, Corkscrew Willow and the flowering Cranberry bush. Or plant my favorite, the Beautyberry bush. This bush sprouts deep purple berries in the fall and retains them all winter. It looks like a Christmas tree with purple bulbs all winter.

LESSONS FROM THE GARDEN: *Seeds of Wisdom for Parents*

# CHAPTER TEN

# AMONG THE ROSES

Proverbs 5:23 (NIV)
"For lack of discipline they will die,
led astray by their own great folly."

"Is there something wrong with that rose?" a friend asked, while she watched me cut back an unruly cane. The vigorous climber was selected to enhance the entrance of my memorial garden. Every spring, I re-direct, tie back, and cut off winter growth.

"No, there's nothing wrong with it that a little pruning won't help tame," I answered.

"But you've cut back so much, how do you decide which canes to tie to the arbor and which ones to chop off?" she asked.

I explained: if the young shoot is healthy and compliant, I can train the canes to grow over the trellis, weaving them among the crossbars of the arch. If instead, it pulls away from the support structure and anchoring it down is unsuccessful, I cut it off. I've tried forcing growth change, only later finding that I have to cut the branch away. In the interest of preferred progress, I now just snip off the offending vine.

After spending many years with plants, I've come to respect each one's unique 'personality'. Rather than work against the natural strength of a plant, I work with it to cultivate it to its best.

"I want this rose to climb over the arch, so I have to show it how," I answered, already aware what her next comment would be.

"I don't think I could cut off such a large, healthy looking shoot," she remarked, as a four-foot branch fell to the ground.

Rookie gardeners always have the hardest time cutting back what looks like vigorous growth. Lack of experience hasn't yet taught them that cutting back actually creates the most vibrant, abundant life in a plant.

"If you don't trim the wild growth, the rogue vines will rob the life from the main plant. By controlling the good growth and giving it direction, the rose stalks will produce abundant blooms."

My friend was skeptical, but I continued, hoping to make my point. "I expect it to show at its best and would be disappointed if it was ragged and looked like a wild blackberry bush. So I trim it and rein in the wild growth to help it produce."

My friend asked the same question I had asked many years ago: "Are you talking about plants or people?"

I was trained for life at the hands of a master many years ago when I was first learning how to be a gardener and a mother. My mentor's lessons began teaching me how or what to do with my flowers, but I always walked away with tidbits on how to parent my children, too.

As my friend and I continued to talk while I worked, I saw the wheels turning in her mind. She is not only a new gardener but also a new mom wanting to be the very best she can be. There is something about the moment we all become mothers (and fathers) that our desires are stirred to be better at parenting than our parents were, yet not to lose all the best things our parents did right. There is something very intimidating about the massive responsibility of shaping another human's life. Our hearts cry out, "What do I do now?"

Like this young mother, I wanted to raise my children to be the very best they could be. I don't care if they are 'the best' in the world's eyes, but I do care that they become their best.

We know they will need a support structure. It takes hard work to help our children understand the strength and support of family.

Was there trimming in the lives of our children? ABSOLUTELY! My mother cut huge ugly rogue sprouts out of my life in order to groom me to adulthood, and we lovingly have been doing the same for our children. It was difficult to trim rowdy sucker canes from their lives. It didn't make us popular. Integrity and strength of character requires shaping and tender loving care, and more times than not—tough love.

Like with my roses, and as an apprentice mom, I was often unsure of what or how much trimming and training to do; but when I was in doubt, I always secured my young vines to the integrity of God's trellis. With much prayer, mentoring advice, and trusting my heart, I learned the unique pliability of each child; and as I did with my roses, I took care to bend them without breaking them.

Most new gardeners feel successful when they see foliage of any kind, but experienced gardeners know even a weed produces abundant growth. Children, left to their own grooming, will produce, but as parents our job must take precedence in determining the influences that will direct them. Without parental direction, our children can become like the wild roses that wander aimlessly.

It is essential for us to weed around our children by pulling bad influences away that threaten to choke their development. Then we need to fertilize them with praise daily to stimulate healthy maturity. It is also sometimes necessary to cut large ugly negative influences from their lives until the day comes when they can battle the elements outside the greenhouse on their own. Many gardeners learn by trial and error.

Unfortunately, the cost of error is too expensive when it comes to our children. Often a master gardener, mentor or 'how-to' book can help us be immediately successful. However, I have found I know my plants best when I spend hours with them on my knees in the garden.

My friend, still watching me cut the wild branches from the rose bushes, asked sincerely, "What if I cut the wrong branches, or cut too much?"

Smiling at her and handing her the clippers, I encouraged, "Just give it a try. If you make a mistake, there is always next month's growth to practice on and they are much more resilient than you think. Don't worry—sturdy, grounded roses will be beautiful in spite of us. The only real mistake you can make is leaving them unattended."

• • •

**Parent Prayer:** Lord, seek out any rogue growth in me and cut it away that I might honor You. Then show me which 'suckers' to cut away from my children's lives that they might also honor You. Give me courage to allow You to cut away wild growth in our children and avoid rescuing them, thus avoiding quenching Your lessons for them.

**Seeds of Wisdom:** Lack of direction when our children are young may for the moment appear cute. We might even think we are fostering independent thinking by allowing them to practice poor manners, lack of respect, lack of follow-through, and being irresponsible. Try to visualize what that behavior will look like as a teenager. Allowing them to be rogue when they're young may actually sap the true growth in their lives and leave them lost and/or shunned by the world they must survive in.

**Garden Tip:** As a rule of thumb, any branch that grows straight up and has minimal leaf growth is a sucker; cut it away. Don't be fooled by false growth or it will eventually kill your roses. Trim them 1/3 back on Columbus Day in the fall, and another 1/3 at Easter. Any branch that can't support the weight of a full blooming rose should be cut away as well.

# CHAPTER ELEVEN

# MOTHER'S AGELESS WISDOM

2 Corinthians 3:2-3 (NIV)
"You yourselves are our letter, written on our hearts, known and read by everybody. You show that you are a letter from Christ, the result of our ministry, written not with ink but with the Spirit of the living God, not on tablets of stone but on tablets of human hearts."

"You just don't understand." I screamed. "You never want me to grow up!" slamming the car door as I got out. My mom quietly sat in the car for several more moments. I could tell she was as frustrated as I was. Our conversations lately were anything but conversations. It seemed we couldn't talk without a battle of wills that ended in a standoff. Mom was old-fashioned and didn't understand things in the real world. I was eager and ready to take on life. I was, after all, almost sixteen.

Time travels forward whether we are ready or not and I have recently completed raising two children and surviving that "almost sixteen" age. I too was told I was old-fashioned and didn't really understand the world today. I can almost see my mom chuckle as I struggled through the same conversations I inflicted on her.

Today I'm sitting in the garden under a large arbor my son and my husband built as a gift for Mother's Day. It's a wonderful place to sit to contemplate the past and the future. I often sought solace here under the arbor following those dreadful discussions with my teens. There were times when we each walked away feeling battered and I wondered if in fact I really was too old-fashioned.

Planted beside the arbor posts are two Chinese Wisteria vines. I remember the day I placed great hopes in them as I covered their roots and faithfully watered them. I could hardly wait to see what maturity would bring.

Prior to planting the precious vines, it was essential to build the arbor they would climb on. We sunk strong weather-resistant posts deep into the ground to support the anticipated weight. We then set solid sturdy uprights to hold the cross boards intended to prop up and maintain the tender new shoots, directing their development. All this planning seemed a bit overdone at the moment these vines were no bigger around than a pencil and only twelve inches long. But I trusted the old gardener I'd bought them from and did as I was told. He warned me to prepare for vigorous growth or the vines would take over the garden destroying anything they could climb over.

Time passed and the little vines grew. Daily, I trained the new growth to lean on the posts for support. Sometimes I had to restrain and other days I had to use my clippers to cut away the wild growth that wouldn't yield to direction. I watched for suckers that needed to be immediately cut away to prevent energy being drained from the new vine. Selectively, I allowed the strong vines to continue, carefully trimmed away the unruly growth, and the wisteria climbed the posts. I wove the vines within the cross boards until they were completely filled in.

Today, I sit beneath its protective cover; not only is the vine strong, but it produces the most amazing purple flowers that hang like heavy grape clusters. Each little vine is now a thick, sturdy tree—so sturdy, in fact it doesn't need the posts any more to support it. If with age and weather the posts fade away, the wisteria will remain upright, solid and sure.

Smiling I realize mothers are much like the posts of my arbor. For a time we support the young vines guiding and directing, pruning and restraining, clipping and watering; stimulating sturdy development.

Mothers and gardeners have a way of placing their dreams and hopes in little shoots but it takes a serious commitment to produce successful blooms. I understand today that my mother was not old-fashioned and truly did understand the world I lived in. I'm thankful she was diligent to restrain, retrain, water and prune my life. Her support of me was the post that directed my life. And although my gratefulness may be many years late, I am thankful for her efforts on my behalf.

My heart was warmed this year to hear from my own children that although they at the time hated my restraints, they are thankful I cared enough to cultivate the best in them.

I pray that one day my children's children will praise their efforts in parenting. I pray that when my children are parents, they will lovingly prune and stand firm in order to be a sturdy post for my grandchildren.

But for the moment, I giggle with secret delight when I realize my children will have children who will slam doors and call them old-fashioned. Perhaps we'll share a seat on my bench, under the wisteria vine as I remind them of the secrets of the ageless vines. We'll laugh together as I tell them that although maturing children into adults is tough, their children, too, will survive their parenting.

• • •

**Parent Prayer:** Lord, help me to parent Your children, Your way! Teach me to be tender and tough like You are with me.

**Seeds of Wisdom:** Take special pictures of you with each of your children and hang them through the house. When they reach the age where they want more independence and don't like anything we say, the pictures will serve as roots while they try their wings. We have several digital photo frames that scroll through special memories. On the days when they hate you, move the photo frames to new places in the house so they'll notice them again, and then pray for patience and meet them on the other side of adolescence.

**Garden Tip:** If you should build an arbor for a climbing Wisteria vine, plant the post deeply (at least 18") in concrete or a metal casing to avoid rot. In a short time, the vine will be very heavy; be certain the support structure can bear up under the weight.

# CHAPTER TWELVE

# A CHIME SONG

Jeremiah 29:11 (NIV)

"For I know the plans that I have for you,' declares the LORD, 'plans for welfare and not for calamity to give you a future and a hope.'"

The melodious song of a flawlessly tuned wind-chime drifts over the garden. The symphony of harmonious strains compels the kind of listening acknowledges a change in the wind. This particular chime only sounds when the wind moves from the north to the south, suggesting a change in the weather. Led by an invisible conductor, the variations in the strains invite my spirit to halt briefly.

Sometimes in the hustle and bustle of survival living, continued existence can take on the pace of endure or die. A fast pace, as it often does, can quench our spirits and cause us to forget to ask the 'what if' questions. Routines can choke out fresh ideas and fear chases dreams to the back edges of our mind categorizing them as some day thoughts.

As September ushers in the new school year, parents and teachers share the blessed responsibility of cultivating teens into grown-ups. In order for these adolescents to metamorphosis into adults, we must help them to grasp the lessons designed to mature them. Again this year, as my incoming students arrive in the classroom, I will ask them to create a "Things to do before I die" list. Putting goals on paper helps students to focus on expecting big dreams for themselves.

I think that too often as instructors, we desire our wisdom to be passed on as if we'd learned to play it perfectly the first time. However, if the truth were told, before we mastered our song, we misplayed many notes until we learned to construct a harmony accurately representing us—a soul song that we and only a handful of loved ones recognize as ours.

If I could breathe wisdom from the rich music of my life into the future of these students, it would include: shun apathy, run from procrastination, believe in your dreams and embrace the changes life sends your way. Without playing wrong notes, the right notes will never feel true. I'd encourage them to experience the sharp notes and the flat ones so that when they strike a perfect harmony they will know its 'rightness'.

Change can be the scariest, most unsettling, exciting learning event in our life. It challenges complacency, tests our limits and pushes our passion to new levels. Most people fight against change and allow anxiety to win the 'what if' game. Research statistics tell us that 100 percent of people dream dreams for their life, but only two percent actually dare to live their dreams.

Recently, I received a great compliment from my son who said, "Mom, I admire you; you're fearless." I wasn't always. I think all of us have fears; I know I do. But my fear comes from a different place. I fear not trying rather than trying and failing. I take risks, but they are calculated risks. It would be selfish of me to leave my life for others, to manage. However, once the safety factors such as life, finances, worth, health and others are accounted for, I'm willing to jump off the cliff to see if my wings will hold me. I refuse to live a life of regret fueled by the fearful 'what if' monster. I would rather wrestle with the ogre of angst and dare to walk the forbidden forest of someday thinking—today.

Recently at my birthday party, a gathering of family and friends toasted some of my achievements. None of my accomplishments are big enough that they will ever win a Pulitzer Prize, but I was surprised and moved to know my 'cliff jumping' had positively affected others. At that moment, all the off-key notes I'd struck didn't seem to matter as much as the chords I'd learned to play.

The musical of chimes over the garden brings my thoughts back to earth and to the business of planting and watering. But, for one brief moment, I thought I could hear someone else sounding the chime, blending a new song mixed with chords from my own opus.

● ● ●

**Parent Prayer:** Lord, teach me to listen for Your song, that I might be able to accept the winds of change and sing Your praises. Help me to place Your song in Our children's heart(s) so they will know Your voice, Your familiar song, and learn to sing with You.

**Seeds of Wisdom:** It's good to know your child's fears and encourage them to challenge them. Some children will excel at challenging themselves and some will need to be placed in safe situations to ensure success until they build the courage to try harder things. Creating mini-successes balanced with stretching themselves to do more difficult things will help to round out our children.

**Garden Tip:** Adding a wind-chime of your liking adds another layer of restfulness and welcome tones to your garden. Be sure to listen to the chimes in the store before bringing them home; their tones are unique to themselves as well as to each person's liking.

# LESSONS FROM THE GARDEN: *Seeds of Wisdom for Parents*

# CHAPTER THIRTEEN

# A GOOD RUN

Matthew 25:23 (NIV)

"His master replied, 'Well done, good and faithful servant! You have been faithful with a few things; I will put you in charge of many things. Come and share your master's happiness!"

I breathe the distinct smell of a wood-stove being stoked to ward off the early morning chill. The sun over the hillside wearing a coat of many colors to dazzle those committed enough to rise early. The morning dew sparkles on a spider's web, inviting me take a closer look. My morning walks are intentionally brisk in order to warm the air between my sweatshirt and my t-shirt underneath. I walk with the sleeves of my sweatshirt pulled down over my hands to keep them warm. On the first lap around, my body tempts me to go back to bed, under my quilt to observe the waking world from there. But it is the part of me that needs to be amid the woods and my garden as it wakes up that wins today.

I love my garden during an Indian summer. The competition of brilliant summer flowers in their encore performances blooming next to the deep rich fall colored showstoppers leaves me breathless. The swan song of the exiting beauties dares the fall buglers to out-shine them. It is the time of year when I start the day in long pants and an oversized sweater and by noon I'm shedding down to shorts and a t-shirt. The days require sunglasses and the nights need quilts.

Sounds change from the whirl of lawn mowers to the dry crunching of leaves under a rake. Grilled steaks become soups and summer fruits go to sleep with the "ping" of a canning jar lid. The autumn leaves wave their final good-byes to the tree as they make their way to the ground. Their end is somehow familiar and comforting. Comforting because we know the seasonal cycle will continue despite our understanding of it or our ability to control it. Fall, as with the other seasons, stands as a reminder that as powerful as we think we are, we are not allowed a say in the beginning or the ending of the seasons of our lives.

I trust a sovereignty infinitely more powerful and in charge of making these life-altering decisions. He alone determines the day I will be discharged from my earthly responsibilities.

This fall my memorial garden will gain a new rose in remembrance of a life lived in anticipation of a 'better-than-here' returning home. Our family will choose a rose to honor Grandma's memory. Unfortunately, they still don't make red, white, and blue roses—her favorite color combination; so we will have to settle for a memorable red rose. Grandma's funeral was a celebration because she knew where she was going when she left this earthly realm. She knew her spirit would not be imprisoned and leaving life behind held no fear for her.

Grandma and I had planned for this day years before. We talked about enjoying happy memories after she would be gone from us. We reminisced about her beautiful roses that had grown along the fence of her home. Her garden was one of the first places where I fell in love with flowers. Together, we ordered from a magazine a teacup with flowers on it that she liked, with the promise that, when she emancipated herself from this life, it would then return to me and be added to my teacup collection. In this way, her memory can still be a part of my garden tea parties.

As this season comes to a close and time quickly marches on, I think I'll plant her memorial rose in the garden where I can see it daily from my kitchen window. I want to live my life each day as one who embraces, enjoys and completes my life's purpose. And like Grandma, I can confidently exit saying, "I've had a good run; I can go now."

• • •

**Parent Prayer:** Lord, help me to live my life in such a way that when We meet face to face You will say to me, "Well done, good and faithful servant." Help me to be worthy of, "her children will rise up and call her blessed," so they too will desire your praises.

**Seeds of Wisdom:** Often times, it helps to start training our children with the end in mind. List what character traits and family values are important for your child to learn. Decide what that trait will look like at 18, 16, 13, 10, 8, 5 and 3 years-of-age. Then begin to discuss how to move in that direction at each interval. This strategic planning helps weed out the unnecessary no's and helps parents define the boundaries and consequences. Doing this also helps parents to not worry over the little things.

**Garden Tip:** Some of the best moments in the garden are over a shared cup of tea. My collection of tea cups is intentionally eclectic. I purchase teacups that I like at garage sales and estate sales particularly if I know the woman who owned them enjoyed her friends and family. This way, an essence of her can remain in my garden having tea.

# CHAPTER FOURTEEN

# EMPTY NEST

Isaiah 40:31 (NIV)

"But they that wait upon the LORD shall renew their strength; they shall mount up with wings as eagles; they shall run, and not be weary; they shall walk, and not faint."

Two days before my son's high school graduation I stood in the garden pouting. I realized I didn't know how to completely let go of mothering him. When our daughter left home, I clung to the knowledge I still had the youngest to fuss over, but this time my nest would be empty.

While sitting on one of the flowerbed walls, immersed in my self-pity, a baby bird fell with a "plop" from the maple tree near me. Its mother was screaming a tirade of warnings while jumping from limb-to-limb above me. Forgetting my self-indulgence, I ran to help the baby bird before my cat made a quick lunch of him.

His body was as round as a tennis ball. His wings were half covered in feathers and half covered in down. It looked as if he'd chosen to leave the nest just a week or two too early. When I reached to pick him up, he greeted me with an expectant open mouth. Realizing I wasn't his mother, his squeaks brought a scolding from the mother robin that made me fear for my life. The nest was too high in the tree to return him. I gently placed him in the covered platform bird feeder about seven feet off the ground, safe from predators. I moved away to watch what the mother robin would do.

His mother continued to bounce from limb to limb calling to him as he teetered on the edge and jumped out, again landing with a thud on the soft ground under the heather. Replacing him in the feeder, I heard the mother robin change the pitch and frequency of her song. This time instead of jumping, he looked for her and calmed down. She amazed me by continuing her vigil for three hours.

I felt as if I was that mother in a similar situation. I couldn't put my own son back in the nest and I wasn't completely convinced yet that his wings were mature enough to enter the world.

She continued to call to her chick from several locations in the yard as the baby bird watched her every move. First she called from a rose trellis, next from a lower rock wall where the baby bird had to stand up to see her. Then she moved to the grass, just far enough away that he had to move to the edge of the feeder to continue to see her. All the time she was making these strategic moves, she never stopped calling out to him.

Moving farther and farther away in the yard, she began to pull worms from the ground. The baby robin apparently could not stand the increasing distance anymore and began to shout back to her. When he neared what appeared to be a panic stage, she relented and flew to the feeder to comfort him. But in less than a minute she stood on the edge of the feeder, looking back over her shoulder at him, calling out an encouragement while returning to the yard. This scenario repeated itself several more times as she encouraged him to take to the air and fly . . . which he did.

From watching her, I learned that once the time had come for my baby to fly, my job was to recognize it and shout encouragement. From a distance, the lesson of letting go appeared uncaring, but was the last most important "equipping" lesson for successful flight.

I realized from her example, flight was a choice, not a chance. She could not do it for him. Since he had made the decision to leave the nest, ready or not, her function then was to teach him to fly. Like it or not, the baby bird was out of the nest and her job description had changed.

I have to remind myself flight training is necessary to avoid the predators in life waiting to devour a rookie stepping into adulthood. By hanging on to my young adult, I would guarantee his lack of survival. At this time in his life, my "letting go" is the last selfless labor of love that will set my child's wings to flight.

I pray he will soar with eagles!

• • •

**Parent Prayer:** Lord, teach me to find the balance between bringing my grown children back to the nest and calling them to flight. And before they leave home, Lord, help me to build their wings strong enough that they may handle soaring!

**Seeds of Wisdom:** Long before children leave home, it is essential that we allow them to be involved with people, activities, and opportunities to try their wings and fail. They need positive experiences with others as well as the balance of negative experiences. Failing and picking yourself back up is best learned before they leave home so we have the opportunity to direct their thinking. Kids that never fail, often fail as adults because they lack the experience.

**Garden Tip:** Have plenty of bird houses, bird baths and bird food in your garden. The bird songs alone are reason enough, but taking time to watch their lives is priceless.

# LESSONS FROM THE GARDEN: *Seeds of Wisdom for Parents*

# CHAPTER FIFTEEN

# THE PONO WAY

Titus 2:7-8 (NIV)
"In everything set them an example by doing what is good.
In your teaching show integrity, seriousness and soundness of speech
that cannot be condemned, so that those who oppose you
may be ashamed because they have nothing bad to say about us."

Every garden has a pace, a feel, a rhythm that uniquely defines it. Some gardens feel formal, others wild and unruly, and some spark reverence and meditation. I often visit gardens that leave me awestruck by their masterful craftsmanship and those that embrace the heritage, charms of days long past. My garden is neither formal nor can it brag of great craftsmanship; rather she is at times unruly, but she always delights me with her arms flung wide waiting to welcome me home like a long lost friend.

My husband and I had the opportunity to spend a week in Maui to relax. While my husband surfed, I enjoyed the warm tropical sun on a blanket. Camped out for the week on the beach at a spot, known to locals as Grandma's, was a native family celebrating their birthdays. In typical island spirit, we were quickly adopted and treated like long-lost family. In truth, this is the way we remembered our island paradise where we grew up and we are thankful Hawaii still exists in the hearts of her people.

It didn't take us long to give up the 'tourist' mentality and spend six of our seven days in this same campsite with these new friends. Pikael, the matriarch of the family, and I felt like instant kindred spirits as we talked as easily as if we'd been friends for many years. Our men sat side by side on their surf boards in the ocean, very different in looks, and yet quite similar in hearts. As they talked and road waves together, I could see the years drop away and I saw once again the same high school surfer I'd shared the beach with 30 years ago. I smiled to myself and buried my toes in the sand as I relaxed in an oversized lawn chair.

The day was perfect for sitting, thinking and being committed to doing nothing. David, the head of this family, made his way out of the water and up to the campsite. Dark brown from enjoying the island surf daily, he climbed into the hammock tied between two trees near the shoreline. He said to me, "That man of yours, he stay longer than me."

I looked back out at the huge smile on my husband's face and said, "He's a hard, hard worker, and he knows what it will be like when we return home. He's always loved surfing and it's fun to see him enjoying it so much."

Dave watched him catch a wave and insightfully said, "It's therapy."

"Ummm . . . , you're probably right."

Just about then, a dad and his young son entered the water on a long board. The young boy, probably five or six-years-old, climbed to the front part of the surfboard as his father climbed on behind and they began paddling in tandem out toward the breakpoint. They caught several waves and each time the board surged forward, the father dropped off letting the boy ride the wave. For such a young one, the boy was really good. At the end of the ride, the dad would swim to him as he climbed back onto the board. I watched as this routine went on and on. Dad never spoke a word, but they moved as if they were one surfer together.

After lunch, as the dad and son left the beach, another car pulled in and unloaded three young female surfers. These ladies argued over who would surf first with Grandpa, with the littlest one, no taller than Grandpa's waist, winning the argument. The scene now familiar, repeated itself over and over as each of the three little girls road the waves with Grandpa. I'd been watching for a long time when I commented to Dave, "I don't hear him coaching the girls; they just seem to be quietly enjoying the rides."

Dave smiling a smile much wiser than his years, said, "He's training . . . the Pono way."

I said, "The Pono way?"

Laying his head back onto the hammock, he said, "The Pono way is a way that allows others to feel the 'rightness' without words ... to feel the perfect moment to catch the wave or pass it up. You don't talk about it, you allow them to feel what you feel. It keeps things from being complicated with words and actually lets the ocean teach them to respect her. The island wants to teach us its rhythm so when our lives are out of sorts, we'll recognize it when we return. And she always calls us back to her. We all have to find our own way, make our mistakes, but she always calls us back."

Dave's insight gave me much to think about as I watched the children simply 'be' with the ocean. There were no words of coaching, no cheering fans, no uniforms to denote a team, no instruction manual, no clear boundary lines. There was however the ever-present power of the ocean that reminded the child, "I am your friend, but respect me." The prize was actually catching a wave, no trophies, just the successful mirroring of the teacher.

Returning home, I purposed to bring the Pono way home with me, to share it with the precious students I teach and their parents. My heart aches at how many times our feeble attempts to empower our children fail, because I know, without a doubt, it is a parent's desire to raise their children to be all they are intended to be. So, with our good intentions we push them, sign them up for every conceivable opportunity available and help them strive to 'get ahead'. To protect them we attempt to remove every obstacle in their pathway, often robbing them of valuable chances to learn natural consequences—life university lessons. But mostly, we talk them practically to death, or at least until they completely tune us out and would rather seek out friends, my space, text message or get lost in their Ipod music. Yesterday I asked my students how often they sit around the dinner table without a TV or other distractions so they could talk to each other. It was sad to hear that only two of the twenty-five families eat meals together regularly and worse yet, one high school student said honestly, "If we did that, we'd have to really learn how to talk to each other."

If I had to do it again I'd imitated the Pono way with my children, I would spend more quiet time cuddled under a blanket at midnight watching the stars and sitting on riverbanks making daisy chains while we take turns watching a bobber. Or maybe we'd spend more time in a hammock with a huge pile of books, or take the time to count the seconds between thunder and lightning. I would be more comfortable with silence and making eye contact with one another. I'm trying to learn to listen and to be slower to give my opinion so my children have a chance to measure their ideas aloud. With my students now, I'm trying to find ways to slow the pace of their world. Young people do think, and their thoughts are deep world-changing thoughts, if they have the time to be still. They live in a hurry-up world that clamors noisily at them, robbing them of the valuable processing time.

I go to my garden to rest, to compost the matters of my mind, to feel the sun on my back, to hear the familiar scolding of the birds sitting in the empty feeder, and to realign the speed of my life. My garden doesn't care how long my 'to do' list is, she'll wait. Gardens don't care if we're rich or poor, revered or shunned, healthy or ill; she eventually brings everyone who visits to their knees.

My garden, like the ocean, is where I have been molded in the Pono way. I often stray or ignore her lessons of 'rightness' but she patiently calls for my return. She doesn't chide me when I go because she knows I'll be back. And she's right. She's taught me to seek my Maker's quiet place externally and internally. The ocean, and my garden hold the fingerprints of the true Master here within my reach to give me a place to be still, figure out my problems and my next step in life with Pono power or rightness of heart.

• • •

**Parent Prayer:** Lord teach me Your way; the way of love, patience, kindness and long-suffering. Train me to be sensitive to the power of rightness and to know the destructiveness of being wrong. If I can embrace the lessons, I can also teach them by showing rather than telling.

**Seeds of Wisdom:** In this hurry-up world we live in, children are often denied time and space to just be alone with their thoughts. Plan for times when they are electronically disconnected. Be careful not to allow their time to be filled with so many activities that they don't know how to be alone or know how to entertain themselves with nothing. Don't buy all the newest games and toys. Help them learn to be creative with a cardboard box and crayons, a blanket for a tent or cape, and caps and rocks. When they can be happy with little to nothing, they'll appreciate when they have more than that.

**Garden Tip:** Spending time often in a garden is the perfect way to learn lessons of 'rightness', so plan for wandering in your garden by informal meandering pathways. Place benches and low walls in many places to encourage lingering. Place small tables and chairs in tucked away spots to entice your guests to sit a while.

# CHAPTER SIXTEEN

# HARSH WINTERS ... TOUGH TIMES?

Ephesians 5:15-17 (NIV)

"Be very careful, then, how you live—not as unwise but as wise, making the most of every opportunity, because the days are evil. Therefore do not be foolish, but understand what the Lord's will is."

I remember during the recession of the 80s, sharing dinner with our friends. We combined our macaroni and cheese packages, with their butter, milk and hot dogs. We shared a meal with a new sense of the word 'shared'. If you talk to the four kids between us, they didn't know we were struggling to put food on the table, they only remember that we ate together, played games, and had a picnic on the floor of the living room.

We played unorganized baseball and magically every neighborhood child along with their dads found our backyard. The neighborhood echoed with screams and laughter. And no one knew that we didn't have enough.

We lost our home in '86, moving the four of us, two dogs and a cat, into a seven hundred-square-foot trailer. We fed the four of us on $120 a month, and made a game of shopping together as a family, splitting up the grocery list to see who could do it the fastest and save the most money. We had family nights and no TV. We did not own a computer, cell phones, 4-wheelers, video games, label clothing, new cars or enjoy fast foods. We swam in the creek, read books, sat down to dinner together every night, baked cookies with grandma, knew our neighbors, canned foods together, and we talked.

## We talked.

Our family isn't perfect. We've had our bumps, bruises, and made our mistakes, but we value that through every tough time in our home, we've gone through it together as a family. It is my firm belief that we are strong because we weathered tough times together. During the worst of times, we learned to make it the best of times.

This past winter was especially hard on my garden. My things-to-do list is longer than usual. I've listed which plants survived, which ones need more attention, which plants need to be moved, who needs to be propped up, replanted, or just thrown away. The harsh winter killed some of the less than hardy plants and still others that I tried to trick into thinking they could grow in this zone have been almost irreparably burned by the frost. Hard winters in the garden—much like our own hard times—teaches us to be more vigilant, more prepared, and less caught up in things that will not last.

If you talk to the old timers who have weathered economically difficult times, wars, and world crisis, they'll often tell you some of the best times in their lives happened during the worst times of their lives. When jobs and money run scarce, we often discover we can do with less, we learn to ask for help, and we become more aware of reaching out to others. We may reconnect with our neighbors, learn the joy and value of bartering, and discover what 'things' in our life we've been running, versus what things have been running us. Possessions become less important and are replaced by the value of people and relationships.

**"I'm convinced, whatever can be taken away from you, cannot be who you are."** Paul Young, author of *The Shack*

During harsh times, families go back to dinners at home, less time is spent in the car running here and there, and vacations become moments captured every day rather than two weeks 'away'. It seems during tough times, families and friends draw closer together. Birthdays and weddings, funerals and graduations become much more important for us to attend and the Sunday afternoon potluck is the highlight of the week.

One of the reasons I love old gardens best is because they have weathered the test of time and storms. It's easy to see that a rookie garden won't last if the gardener doesn't continually tend to it, but an old garden will go on blooming in spite of the missing gardener. A plant that is brilliantly gorgeous has probably been moved, had the dead wood cut out of it, and had enough manure thrown on it to become its best . . . ; and it has learned to weather the storms without wilting.

Like old gardens, people—families—gain growth individually and collectively, perhaps for the first time developing deep roots in order to survive the difficult times. Perhaps hard times make us tough, but I believe they build the kind of strength that cultivates lasting hardiness and vitality—the kind that can weather even the worst storms.

• • •

**Parent Prayer:** Teach me, Lord, to be content in simple things—Your things—the things that really matter. Then help me to instill this contentment in our children. Teach them to value wise counsel and to seek truth above all else.

**Seeds of Wisdom:** We built a circle of five around each child made up of five other people they could count on to go to in times of trouble, for counseling or when they just couldn't talk to mom and dad. In that circle of five, we always included elderly adults. Senior citizens' values and life experiences are rich in lessons our children cannot get anywhere else. They may lend a perspective that is far wiser than we can give to our child.

**Garden Tip:** I love to trade plants with other gardeners. When winter approaches, we dig up our excess bulbs and swap them with other gardeners. Each time they bloom, I remember who it was that gave it to us and the circumstances surrounding it. Now when I walk through my garden, it is full of blooming memories!

# CHAPTER SEVENTEEN

# NEVER UNDERESTIMATE

Psalms 139:13 (NIV)
"For you created my inmost being;
you knit me together in my mother's womb."

"It's as good as dead. You might as well just yank that hydrangea out now," I said, so certain of myself.

"Honey, I tried to just trim it, but the branches are as big around as my arms." My husband had spent the better part of an hour removing a cranberry bush that over the years had grown into a view-blocking monster of a tree. It was supposed to be a dwarf bush—but it was comparable in size to the tree that stands nearby.

Complaining loudly now, I attempted to educate my husband on the destruction he had unknowingly just committed. "The cranberry bush was shading the hydrangea. Now the hydrangea will fry in the sun. You might as well pull it out, too; it will never produce under these conditions."

I have babied a hydrangea given to me nearly twelve years ago. I've deep-watered the roots, kept it shaded from the end of the days' hot summer sun, and fed it just the right amount of nutrients to turn the large flower heads a deep blue and purple. I've waited patiently all this time with hopes it would produce in massive quantities. Each year I've been rewarded with one more flower head than the year before. This year I was expecting 8-10 blooms.

"I didn't know that," replied my husband. "Why don't we just leave it there this year and see if it makes it? If it doesn't, then I'll pull it out." I returned to trimming my roses and, still pouting, turned my back on him and thought 'you non-gardener'. I knew he felt bad, but I honestly believed all my hard work had just been destroyed and I'd have to explain to the friend who had given the old homestead plant to me why it hadn't survived after blooming profusely for her, in their yard.

Not too many years ago, I learned a valuable lesson regarding making character judgments on other people. I take my role in the human race very seriously. As human beings, we have the power to set another persons' life on a positive flight or into a destructive spiral by the way we treat each other, the words we say, the models we set and the praise we give or don't give away. At times in my haughty way, I have said things that were less than kind about someone else. One instance, years ago, I made a comment to a colleague about the lack of a student's ability. As if I could know all things, I said, "It's sad that most students' floor will be this student's ceiling." Dressed up in politeness, I underestimated a child long before he'd even had a chance to prove himself to the world.

This comment felt like a prediction and I immediately wished I'd never said it. But there it was out there beyond my unfiltered lips. In my embarrassment and shame, I began to pray that God would allow me to see what He saw, and to make right my unkind words. Even though the student never knew what I had thought, I made a point to pray regularly for him, and to try to anticipate help that might be needed for his success.

In spite of me, this student went on to be very successful, highest ranked in his class, the winner of many national awards, married and is raising a wonderful family. I'm so glad I wasn't right. I'm so glad he never knew my unkindness, my underestimation of him. His life taught me the power of words, the value of never underestimating anyone for any reason at any time. With new found humility, I strive now to believe the best, speak the best, and be the first to applaud success.

Unfortunately, it seems I have to be continually reminded, like the lesson my husband and the hydrangea taught me this summer . . . ; did I mention that this year with the extra sunlight, there are over 50 huge purple blooms on it?

• • •

**Parent Prayer:** Lord, remind me often that You NEVER

underestimate me, and I need to see Our children as You see them, and to NEVER underestimate their ability to understand and be what you've planned for their lives.

**Seeds of Wisdom:** Our children are now adults and if I had to do it again, I would listen more than talk. We need to hear out their ideas, allowing them to measure them aloud. I would NOT make futuristic evaluations about things I have no way of knowing as fact. If we praise to the level you want them to rise to, they will. Ex.-It's not like you to get angry over nothing, can you tell me what's going on?

**Garden Tip:** When planting new plants, take the time to read up on their ideal growing conditions. This will save you lots of frustration and money by allowing them to be planted in their best growing environment.

# LESSONS FROM THE GARDEN: *Seeds of Wisdom for Parents*

## CHAPTER EIGHTEEN

# PASSING ON THE BLESSING

Hebrews 10:23 (NIV)
"And let us consider how we may spur one another on toward love and good deeds."

"If you build it without a proper foundation it will sink." I could hear my husband out in the garden, coaching my son on the merits of building a concrete rock wall. The wall is three feet tall and has an eight-foot diameter. It was built to surround a five-foot stone statue named Rebecca, who stands guardian over our garden. The wall restrains yards of dirt that is home to 300 tulips in the spring and 100 marigolds in the summer.

The ground where the wall is built was the base of an old decayed maple tree, so it was necessary to spread a layer of gravel before leveling each brick. The work is tedious and hard. My son had been working intensely for over an hour when I overheard the corrective instruction. "Without the gravel to prevent the settling of the stones, they will sink and the wall won't be level," his father encouraged. With this information, my son returned to work on the remainder of the wall.

I watched their conversation from the hammock in the yard. I'd been relaxing in it with another of my "self-help" books. I've read wheel barrows full of books on developing myself into a better person. I've studied how to bring out the best in others, and how to perfect my parenting skills. Studying the wisdom of the Bible, I've found timeless tips regarding how to stir up love and encourage people.

During the days before the birth of Christ, there was a practice known as 'passing on the blessing' to family members. The blessing consisted of the father meeting with the children. There are specific directions for passing on the blessing with the oldest son. By placing their hands on the receiver, words of praise were spoken, and the family inheritance was passed on to the next generation. There were celebrations at many special events and words of praise and prediction were spoken to the recipient. It was a person's birthright, a coming-of-age inheritance. Words that needed to be spoken were spoken. You knew where you stood in your family and in your community.

In our world today, it's not common practice to get mushy and tell people how wonderful they are unless you're Hallmark, or in the early stages of a courtship. I've often been at funerals where everyone took an opportunity to stand up and tell the audience what a wonderful person the deceased was. I always walk away feeling like it's sad that we have to be dead to get people to say the words we would have climbed mountains to hear. It makes me wonder if I could convince my friends and family to have my funeral now while I'm still here and can enjoy their comments. I would enjoy having a blessing passed on to me, and I know I love the look on peoples' faces when I tell them they are special to me.

Ten years ago our family took a trip across the United States and spent several days with my husband's family. It was fun to spend time hearing and seeing where my husband had grown up. The childhood stories they told were wonderful and I watched as my children realized their father had once been their age, too. This was a precious time for all of us. One of the events earmarking a life change for my husband is the day my father-in-law passed on the blessing. During a fishing trip, he shared how proud he was of my husband and the way he had built his family. Although the Vincent men don't have the market cornered on conversation, his words made a profound change in his son, my husband. He has always been a great husband and the world's best dad, but receiving his father's approval completed something in his life. He returned home much more confident and self-assured. His father's words, the simple passing on of the blessing of love and pride for his son, gave my husband a fresh sense of satisfaction and maturity. His Dad was proud of him.

Life is a funny thing: we all need to be encouraged or validated. In fact, most of us go through life trying to find something that makes us feel whole or complete. Some find their confirmation that they are unique by owning lots of material things. Some find

it in being the champion of games; still others strive to be the most successful at something important in their eyes, whatever they deem success is. But I learned from my father-in-law that success has no meaning if there's no one to say "well done."
I also learned from him that words are powerful. They have an ability to set someone free, to encourage someone to fight when they'd rather quit, and to cause a spirit to soar like a falcon as it gives itself up to the sky.

The garden wall was completed with each stone leveled upon a layer of gravel. The wall is perfect still, many years later, except for the four-foot section where the stones were laid without the benefit of the pebble barrier. The section without the gravel has sunk slightly and every year we discuss how it needs to be corrected. And every year we decide it is too difficult to now go back and repair the section. So it stands slightly sagging next to the others. To an architect it's not perfect, but no one will remember the imperfections 20 years from now. What I will remember is the look on my son's face when his dad praised his efforts and said, "Wow, son, you did a great job! I'm proud of you."

As time passes, I don't want the wall repaired. It serves as a reminder to me that if I do not build a strong foundation of love and praise with my friends and family, in time they too may sag under the weight of the world. I want to live within my circle of influence attentive to the thought that our days are numbered, 'Do they know how I feel about them? Have I said all the things they need to hear?'

Don't wait until the funeral. Let the passing on of the blessings begin with ME, and YOU. Our convictions to demonstrate to our children how to live life in an upright, honest and successful manner, is what gives hope to our homes and our community. When we speak our hearts in words and deeds, families are loved, cities are safe and nations are stronger.

• • •

**Parent Prayer:** Lord, elbow me when I need to be quick to praise and close my mouth when I'm too quick to be critical.

**Seeds of Wisdom:** There is great power in words. Every day find something to praise your children and spouse about even if you have to look hard to find it. When you have a complaint sandwich it like a cookie—praise, complaint, praise. You'll accomplish more this way and daily pass on the blessings.

**Garden Tip:** Raised beds and garden walls really enhance the garden on a multi-visual level. In the Northwest, we need to use brick due to the abundance of rain. Build a wall, and talk about the value of a proper foundation with your children while you're building it. As their teen years approach, they'll remember the 'hands-on' lesson.

# CHAPTER NINETEEN

# FEARFUL OR FEARLESS PARENTING?

Proverbs 22:6 (NIV)

"Train a child in the way he should go, and when he is old he will not turn from it."

I heard my husband call me from the backside of the house. He was attempting to spread bark dust in a flowerbed where the ten-foot-tall honeysuckle vine supported by an eight-foot-tall obelisk trellis had blown over during the last windstorm. As I rounded the end of the house, I could see the vines were threatening to take over the nearby blueberry bushes and were keeping my husband from spreading the bark dust.

Try as I may, I could not get the honeysuckle covered trellis to stand back up. To right it, I had to hack away at the nine feet of growth and pull up the extra roots. When I was finished with the job, the framework was upright, the blueberry was cleared of invading growth, and the honeysuckle cuttings were ready to be discarded. All that remained on the trellis were four main honeysuckle shoots about a foot-to eighteen-inches tall. Thankfully, it is spring; the warming summer air will aid in their survival.

Along with garden repairs and maintenance this time of year, families are preparing for graduations as several levels of 'coming of age' events earmark our calendars. Our children have survived and passed through unique seasons of their lives. This might be the year you send your teen off to college, a marriage, the military, or to experience grown-up life in general.

For many parents, this season can be the most fearfully rewarding time in life. I was scared to death as my two left home; I worried that I hadn't prepared them well enough, or that we'd over-protected them and they would be eaten up by the world. I was concerned that I might have forgotten a crucial lesson, that I might not have said the right thing, or that I had said the right thing and they didn't hear it. I was apprehensive that they might have decided I was 'old-fashioned' and they discounted my words of wisdom. I wrestled with wanting to save them from the cruelties of the world, but also wanting them to have sustainable calluses for the journey before them. I white-knuckled my support from a distance, secretly wanting to 'fix' every problem they encountered, yet knew that weathering storms in life is essential to maturity, self-reliance, and the peace of knowing you 'can'. As parents watching our charges grow, we weathered their storms of "I'm eighteen and you can't tell me what to do" with some semblance of grace. But I remember clearly the moment of letting go and trust that they had caught all the parenting lessons we struggled to teach them.

Often while teaching, I encounter well-meaning parents who love their children so much, they have strategically, and devotedly, created situations where their children will be successful. I applaud those efforts. However, as their charges grow, those parents often think if their children avoids failure or negative situations they will be better adults, and in fact I've found the opposite to be true. It is essential that teens learn the tough lessons of failure and survival prior to experiencing disappointments without a safety net.

When our young adults encounter fiascos in life, if they are still living at home, we parents will have the opportunity to debrief the lessons with our children and encourage them with a 'how could you have handled this differently' conversation. It is the trying and failing before becoming successful that teaches inexperienced young people that In the future all will be O.K. This way when grown children struggle as adults, they'll have some experience to lean on.

I looked at my honeysuckle as it hangs limp and wimpy from its lattice base, now only a mere shadow of what it had been.

"Wow! You really cut that back; will it survive?" my husband asked in concern.

"Yes, she is experienced at this; her roots are strong and she has been cut down and moved three times before today. She knows what to do," I assured him.

As with the care I put into growing my honeysuckle, parents need to establish strong roots in their young people and provide sturdy trellises for them to lean on when hormonal teens don't choose to lean on their parents. When our children were young, my husband and I encouraged relationships with five other people who we knew would give them the sound advice we would when, as teens, they sought them out to talk. We made it clear what our desires were with these 'supports' so that their advice would follow our values and hopes for our children. This also meant we had to trust the support structure we'd placed around them. As we expected, there were times when our teens didn't talk to us and their 'supports' were ready for them.

But mostly, we tried to share and model for our children the measuring stick we held ourselves accountable to, much like a plumb line for a carpenter. Our plumb line is our faith in Christ. Every parent, along with their children, will have to decide what guideline to measure up against. But I have to share that with Christ as our plumb line, and the Scriptures as our anchors to hang on to, we often claimed and still claim today the verse that says: "Train up a child in the way he should go: and when he is old, he will not depart from it" Proverbs 22:6 (KJV).

Did you notice the gap between child and old? There is a lot of room for young adults to make mistakes until they are old, but as a parent I'm focusing on the 'when they are old they will not depart from it'. I take great comfort in knowing that my measuring stick has an owner's manual for these young adults which includes the steadfast promise, we can shout back to Christ in reverent reminder of His job now that we are no longer the 'owners' of our children's lives. It is this confidence that allows me to sleep at night embracing fearless parenting rather than fretful sleep and fearful parenting. And, like my honeysuckle, when the disasters of living life occur in our children's lives and they are struck down, they will know from prior experience how to rely on their roots and re-produce growth.

• • •

**Parent Prayer:** Lord, train me that I might be a good trainer for Your children and that they will learn to lean on You. Help me to train them so one day they will train their children Your way.

**Seeds of Wisdom:** Sometimes our children learn more from knowing what not to do rather than from always doing things right. Allow them the room to fail at tasks and one of two things may happen: 1) They'll learn valuable lessons about themselves, their expertise, their limitations and the value of teamwork, resources and properly pre-assessing the situation or 2) They'll accomplish the task!

**Garden Tip:** When planting a 'climber', build the frame that they will climb on sturdy enough that it is able to withstand aggressive growth. You'll also want to build the support out of durable material that will not rot or crumble under the future growth.

# CHAPTER TWENTY

# IRRITATION OR INSPIRATION?

Ephesians 2:10 (NIV)
"For we are God's workmanship, created in Christ Jesus
to do good works, which God prepared in advance for us to do."

"Without continual growth and progress, such words as improvement, achievement, and success have no meaning." Benjamin Franklin

Arriving home from our plant shopping, I pulled my car as close to the garden as I could to make for easier unloading. I'm always surprised at how many plants I can pack into my little car. Today we picked out seventy-two vibrant yellow zinnias, and forty-eight neon red begonias to plant around the fountain.

"Wow! I can't believe how big your plants grow in your garden," my friend said as she admired the hanging baskets on the arbor.

I was busy unloading all the little 4" pots to line them up on the flowerbed wall before we started planting.

"You know," she said a bit perplexed, "we planted the same plants at the same time and mine aren't this big and full. What's your secret?"

"I irritate them so they'll be inspired."

"You what?" she laughed. "Is this another one of your 'lessons'?"

We spent some time laying out the plants in an appealing pattern—not too close so each plant has room to grow and fill in the empty spots, and not so far as to make the circle sparse-looking.

"Now, slide the plant out of the pot and turn it upside down. With your fingernails, scratch the roots just enough to irritate them and then plant it in the hole," I said, showing her as I talked.

"Won't you damage the root system?" she asked, nervous about doing it incorrectly.

"No. See how the roots have grown into the shape of the pot? They've become too comfortable; if you don't scratch the roots, they'll continue in the same pattern—as if they were still in the pot even when they're not—and that will stunt their growth. By irritating the roots, they'll begin to put off new little roots and stretch out into the new area of good dirt. That makes them bigger and stronger."

"Oh my goodness, I've always handled mine so gently and would have thought that scoring and nicking the roots would have killed them," she said surprised.

We got busy planting the prize colors for this year's blooms. She was quiet. I didn't break the silence. I've learned that God meets me in the garden wherever I am in my life and I didn't want to intrude on any lesson He might be sharing with her through this planting process. After a while, she spoke.

"So, when you learned this technique, what lesson did you learn about yourself?"

"I learned to find joy in the irritating events in my life."

"Like?" she asked, looking very contemplative.

"Like: when I struggle, asking for help; when finances dried up, finding joy in the simple things; when the car was totaled, learning to be happy staying home. I learned a lot about myself and what I'm made of when I've gone through the really difficult things. I discovered I'm dependable, hard-working, a gap-stander, and I know who I am. Without the painful and irritating things in my life, I'd have never known this God-given quiet strength. I don't wonder any more who I am. And I like knowing I can be counted on."

My friend just laughed and shook her head, "Well, we've all known that for a long time."

"Thank you. But I didn't. I had to learn it, to feel it within."

She sat on the garden wall still holding a begonia in her hand, "So the irritation was the catalyst for growing outside your comfort zone, like the little plant and its pot?"

"Yes. That's the secret. Scrapes and cuts actually produce bigger, better blooms. I stopped being upset with irritations that force me to grow. Now I spend my time looking for the end of the lesson and allow myself to be inspired!"

• • •

**Parent Prayer:** Lord, remind me often that what I see as irritations and struggles may actually be Your lessons of inspiration for a future blessing. Help me to flee from complaining and instead too find the rainbow in the rain.

**Seeds of Wisdom:** Play the Pollyanna game and try to find good in everything that at first appears negative. Speak it out loud often with your children to inspire them to do the same. "When we find three great things about this bad thing, we'll go to the park!"

**Garden Tip:** If you want prolific growth, be sure to dig the hole twice as large as the plant's root ball, scratch or score the roots slightly and fill the hole with water before you place it in the hole. Your plants will thank you with rapid growth!

# CHAPTER TWENTY-ONE

# THE HEART OF A MOTHER ...

Psalms 139:3 (NIV)

"Sons are a heritage from the Lord, children a reward from Him."

It's not that I hate ducks; I just wasn't crazy about taking home thirteen of them! My husband and two children had enjoyed watching a mother duck home-schooling her thirteen ducklings near the dock. We watched and listened to their mother's calls for them to keep up.

With the weekend, the campground soon filled to capacity, bringing perhaps a few that were less than respectful of the gifts of nature. My children's screams of, "They're killing them," brought me to my feet. Young boys and a dog had terrorized the avian family killing the mother duck and were now chasing the ducklings. My husband had already grabbed the dog out of the water, and chastened the boys.

The rest of the day, our two little ones sat on the dock watching the ducklings swim back and forth calling for their mother. It was heartbreaking to watch and what was a perfect camping trip now had been marred for my tenderhearted animal lovers. As we packed to head home, my two came to me with tear-stained faces pleading, "We can't just leave them by themselves; what will happen to them?" I watched as the little ducklings helplessly floated by the dock where my children had been sitting and tried to explain the survival of the fittest theory that even sounded hollow to my own ears as I said it.

My son, taking my hand in his, announced profoundly, "You could be their mother," and somehow the way he said it even made sense to me. Pausing longer than I should have to win the "we-don't-have-room-for-13-ducklings" defense, I looked into the faces of my own babies and refused to go down in history as the mom who wouldn't take care of the baby ducks.

Time passes and, one at a time, the baby ducklings found new homes save the last two we called Mic and Mack. Mic, the female, quickly became the boss of the yard, telling cats and dogs where they could walk and lie down, while Mack, the lone male, obediently followed his sister everywhere she went.

Every spring, Mic would tediously build a beautiful, soft-lined nest, lay 12-15 eggs, and dutifully sit on them for weeks only to be disappointed annually when nothing hatched. One Easter, after hiding the kid's eggs in the yard, we watched as she rolled one of the hard-boiled eggs toward her nest. We laughed at her antics, but as a mom I identified with her efforts to protect what she thought was a baby. I felt so badly for her gallant care and concern for the Easter egg that I got an idea.

After explaining to our local feed store owner, I had an instant cohort in crime. She collected eggs from several nests, aiding me in my efforts to help this barren lady-duck experience motherhood.

When Mic wasn't looking, we carefully removed all of her unfertilized eggs and replaced them with the new fifteen adopted eggs, hoping at least one would hatch and give Mic her first 'Mother's Day'.

We marked the time and watched expectantly every day for any movement. At last, weeks later, the first babies arrived: two chickens, four mallards, and two bob white quail! The next time we saw her there were more chickens and a turkey. All together, she boasted fifteen babies of various sizes, shapes, makes and models! She was the proudest mom I'd ever seen as she happily parading them through the yard for us to see. It was a brood only a mother could love and she never seemed to notice the differences from one child to another; if she did, she never behaved in such a way to make us think it mattered.

No one was allowed within twenty feet of her new family without having her spread her wings and hiss, as if she possessed the ability to take down an elephant. It was hysterical to see so many colors and sizes obediently following their 'mom'. Not one of them dared to disobey her . . . , for if one of them strayed, they brought upon themselves a wrath of scoldings that made everyone in the yard freeze in their shoes—including me.

As a novice mom myself, I learned so many lessons from her. I watched as she demonstrated unconditional love to all of her babies and just as equally distributed discipline. She worked hard to feed them, but seemed to know the perfect time to insist they do it themselves. She instinctively knew the nest provided protection and was resolute that they remain close to it, until the day she pulled the nest apart, forcing them to move on in the world. We watched as she, without thought for her own safety, threatened to take on our 130 pound Lab/wolf when he got too close to the little ones.

Ahhhh . . . , motherhood! The hardest, most exhausting, blessing God has given to me yet. There is no report card to measure my parenting skills and God is still not in the habit of emailing me directions for them. My children never left a hole in my heart that they couldn't, in one second, fill with a touch of their hand, or a smile on their face. We've ridden roller coasters both physically and figuratively. I've worn the hats of sheriff, coach, jailer and cheerleader—equally. When they look back on their youth, I hope they know I was but a girl myself when I first began my reign. And, if I could ask God for one favor, it would be that their heads would be filled with all the great memories and that the mistakes I made would be wiped from their hearts.

I couldn't wait to be a mother. Now, I pray I did my job well. I pray my children embrace life as whole, happy, people, because of me, and in spite of my short-comings.

## LESSONS FROM THE GARDEN: *Seeds of Wisdom for Parents*

• • •

**Parent Prayer:** Dear Lord, mothering is hard! Show me what really matters and what will matter ten years from now. Bring to mind that training in character and not just demanding obedient robots is really what is needed.

**Seeds of Wisdom:** Hands on parenting means you need to be close enough to see what your children are doing. Make your house the hang out house. Fill the fridge with good things to eat, host cooking projects, craft projects, movie night, theme parties and become homework project central. This way you'll be the person to influence your children's friends.

**Garden Tips:** Including our children and their pets in activities helps to teach responsibility and really endear the garden to the entire family. Ducks were excellent at eating up the slugs, if you didn't mind the duck poop! My grown children still talk about our duck adventure!

# CHAPTER TWENTY-TWO

# I THINK I SAW GOD TODAY

1John 4:19 (NIV)

"We love because he first loved us."

"Do you think it will make it?" my friend asked staring at the new flowering shrub we'd just transplanted from my garden to hers.

"That's why I'm planting it here," I answered, "until it re-establishes its' roots and flourishes on its' own."

"You mean because the soil is better here?" she asked.

"Sort of; it's more about protection," I offered.

The shrub we planted had been well-established and I expected it would do well again after being transplanted. But sometimes the uprooting process can throw even a mature, self-sustaining bush into shock. A little stress can be good for motivating new growth, but overwhelming trauma can do permanent damage.

Today's strategy was to plant the reluctant draftee under the overhanging growth of a mothering Clerodendrum. The shelter of her leaves would provide fortification in the event of rough storms until the little shrub was able to restore itself.

"There's nothing wrong with the bush; it just needs a little encouragement to return to doing what it does well," I shared.

We live in strange times, a country of plenty, but at a time which is not so plentiful. Jobs are scarce and economically plush times aren't. For some of us our security has been shaken; what we thought would always be isn't.

We've gotten so use to being independent we've forgotten that our country and its people were made strong by working together. We've forgotten how to lean on one another—not necessarily how to give, but how to receive. We are proud Americans, but sometimes our shortsighted pride can rob others of experiencing an extended supporting hand.

Have you ever met someone who seems to be able to turn every bad situation into something positive? They are the glass is half-full people of the world. Being laid off from a job becomes an opportunity to do something they've always wanted to do but haven't yet done. A crisis in their life may be the very thing that births protection for many others, such as: M.A.D.D. They are the ones who know when to 'accept the things I cannot change' and they really do possess 'the wisdom to know the difference.' When these people enter a room, others often gain fresh perspective and energy from them, and when they leave us, we are often the better for their having been in our lives. And although none of us have the power to change the difficult or ugly things that enter into our lives, we do have the power to change our attitudes and our reactions.

During the recession in the 80s, it was difficult for our family to have someone pay our electric bill, but we simply weren't in a position to meet the obligation and we couldn't work any harder than we were working. I learned to be grateful. I remember saying when the gift was given, "I don't know what to say," and their reply was, "Thank you is enough; someday you'll pass it on."

Today, it gives me a deep sense of connection and thankfulness to do something for someone else. I relive the times others were kind to me when I pass on a kindness. I saw a man holding a sign up by the freeway entrance that simply read "Hungry." Although he may not remember me, I will forever remember the grateful look of surprise on his face when I stopped and handed him a sack lunch and a gift certificate to McDonalds. I enjoy being able to help when I can, and I am finally paying it forward.

When we are the instigator of random acts of kindness, it screams to the world that we value each other. We can restore a person's view of humanity and perhaps shine a light into their life when it might need a bit of illumination.

Our neighbors next door, our extended family members, the people we work with—they all have a story and some of them might have a bleak one at the moment. It takes a courageous person to be a receiver. Givers are blessed when receivers allow them to pass on the gift they have received; and the moment shared between people is tremendously human. When we behave in such a way that makes us all look more like the 'higher level thinkers' where 'love' dictates our actions, it makes it easier to point to God as our maker rather than just being at the top of the food chain.

"I get it," she said, "The bigger plant will protect the new plant from too much sun, the wind and the snow, right?"

"Yes, but more amazingly, when the tree draws water and nutrients to itself through the soil, the water and nutrients must first pass over the roots of the little bush. So, when the tree feeds itself, it will nurture the bush."

"So the little tree will be paying it forward!" she said.

"Exactly!"

• • •

**Parent Prayer:** Lord, help me to stay in Your refreshing pathway while I remain the protector of Our children. Help me to be sensitive to times when they need my protection and times when they don't, so that they will grow strong enough to also pay it forward.

**Seeds of Wisdom:** Start early with your children with charity giving and volunteering. The benefits for those who receive is minimal compared to the lessons your children will learn about themselves and the world. Volunteer to help with menial tasks like raking leaves, stacking wood, pulling weeds, food banks, animal shelters, and senior centers.

**Garden Tip:** Planting new tender plants near a well-established plant can help build the little plant's strength so that one day it can, itself be moved to a place of supporting.

# CHAPTER TWENTY-THREE

# WILD GROWTH OR FRUIT BEARING?

Colossians 1:10 (NRV)
...So that you may live a life worthy of the Lord and please him in every way: bearing fruit in every good work, growing in the knowledge of God.

Every spring the fruit trees need pruning. We allow them to grow wild all winter, but come early spring, if we want them to bear fruit, the wild growth has to be cut away. Unchallenged, new growth will sap the strength of the budding fruit.

With my ladder perfectly balanced against the tree, clippers in hand, I climb to the level just above the fruit producing branches, and aggressively cut back everything above. I trim selectively in order to protect the young healthy life-giving growth. I notice the branches cut back last year are loaded with full, healthy blooms that will produce fruit this summer.

There's one tree in our yard that we allowed to grow wild and untrimmed. It grew so rapidly that in only a few short years, the branches became a tangled mess. The tree not only produced very little fruit but it grew so quickly, it split in two—killing the tree.

Too often, we as parents, teachers and mentors of young people, get caught up in the world's philosophies which suggest restraining, trimming, curtailing or challenging young people will stunt their development. Yet, it's my experience that the opposite is true. When a child isn't given direction, boundaries and instruction, they become shy, withdrawn and hungry for acceptance. Like water that seeks the easiest path, an immature spirit will look for acceptance in the first place they feel like they belong—which may or may not provide the best future influences.

Children, like trees, thrive when we cut the life-draining suckers from their lives. I'm careful where I prune so as not to bleed the life-giving force, but when I find a fruit-stunting deceiver, I cut it clean from the branch.

Since it is my responsibility to tend the fruit, I must recognize potential threats and remove anything that may weaken my charges. With that in mind, I am best prepared when I am amid the branches, up close. What may look like a gorgeous silhouette from a distance, the pruning is perfected when we are close enough to cut away those things intent on robbing growth.

Sometimes my cutting back causes a shock reaction for a day or two. If I am faithful to choose my timing well, and continue watering, fruit will be produced for all to enjoy and gain inspiration from. Young people, like trees, will be blessed and bless others as well.

**Parent Prayer:** Lord teach me to recognize the difference between trimming and controlling, destructive wild growth verses their personal bent, and to be willing to take a hard line and cut back potential devastation even when it doesn't make me popular.

**Seeds of Wisdom:** Remind yourself often that you won't always like your child but will always love them. That love should guide each decision for your child's present and future growth.

**Garden Tip:** Be familiar with your fruit baring plants. Any branch that grows straight up, unchallenged, will not produce fruit, cut it away. Also remember that slow growth means sturdier roots, trim back rapid or wild growth.

# CHAPTER TWENTY-FOUR

# ONE MORE LESSON BEFORE YOU GO ...

Philippians 3:14 (NIV)
"I press on toward the goal to win the prize for which God has called me heavenward in Christ Jesus."

A wise woman, my friend, taught me much more about myself and life by teaching me about my garden. Today, as I work the soil, I wonder if she would be proud of who I have become thirty years later. I find myself here again today, prayerfully considering my own words of encouragement for the students that will graduate this month. I wonder if I've given them enough preparation to soar on their own wings. I don't want my words to be tangled, or stuffy, arrogant, or condescending. So I ask myself, What would I have wanted to know about life, if I could go back to my own graduation from high school?

Clearing my thoughts and my throat, I address the peonies to practice what I should say. The peonies are good listeners and they tolerate my ramblings as I prepare my one last lesson.

"As you end this journey and begin your first steps of the next, I've prayed long and hard on how to equip you for the trip. What could I pass on that will smooth your journey and enrich your life.

"I cannot tell you what your future will hold, but as I look back over my own life, I can tell you how to prepare for whatever life brings to you. When I say, be prepared for what life brings to you, I mean: what life gives you, what life blesses you with, and what life celebrates with you. But . . . , I also mean what life drags you through, launches you into, crushes you under, presses upon you and trains you for. As much as I'd love your life to be easy and fun, you'll have to forgive me in advance, because I will be praying a dangerous prayer for you. I'll be praying, 'Lord, make them all they can be for You. Lord, do whatever it takes to keep them tied to You, loving You with all their heart.'

"I cannot promise you your lessons will be easy, because we know anything worth having takes hard work. Pick a goal you've yet to complete and focus on it; you'll learn a lot about yourself before you achieve it. Perhaps you'll learn: discipline, consistency, tenacity, and perseverance. I promise you, this obstacle will come up again in your life; save yourself the adult struggle, and embrace the lesson now.

"**Know your Bible:** It will be your plumb line in life—if you know what the Bible says, it will tell you when you are off track, and dance with you when you are on! The power of God's words will inspire you (like a bright light on a dark path), heal you when you need it, comfort you when no one else understands or even cares; keep you company when there is no one else; strengthen you when you are weak; and pick you up one more time than you fall. I want you to be able to discern truth from a lie. If you know God's word, you will have a way to separate the two.

"**Practice Quiet:** Make time to be alone with God and alone with yourself. Make it a habit to still the prattle and noise of the world and hear what you think. Then practice listening for God's voice. Often times, he only whispers. Be there to hear it.

"**Know yourself:** Many adults may live a life lacking joy because they lack purpose. Start today to understand the personal gifts you have been given; this way you will learn where and when to use them. Only then will you find fulfilling purpose in your life.

"**Embrace Pruning:** God prunes those He wants to bear fruit. When your pruning happens (and it will unless you are living your life TOO safe), you will have two choices: whine or consciously ask What am I meant to learn? What am I being trained for? The choice is yours—choose wisely.

"**Learn Boundaries:** I believe everyone wants to be their best, but learn early that our best means we must rest. Even Jesus, who knew he only had 33 years to right the wrongs, took daily time to come apart from people and the world. But from what I've read in Scripture He consistently stopped to spend time in gardens, to eat with friends, and regularly to surround himself with quiet times with His Father. Jesus was not overly busy with empty urgent fruitless tasks. He has taught me, it's ok not to be involved in every activity the world offers or even expects of me. Choose your areas of service carefully, build your boundaries, and don't feel guilty sticking to them. You are no good to anyone unless you are your best for you.

**"Be slow to judge, and quick to Love:** Everyone has a story. We can never know all they have gone through. There is a saying, "People do not care how much you know, until they know how much you care." It has never been more important than today—a world filled with lost and hurting people. Err on the side of love; you'll never be sorry you did.

**"Build Relationships over Preaching:** Earn the right to share Christ with others. If it doesn't work in your own back yard, why should others buy into your message?

"It might sound strange for a teacher to tell you, focus on Christ first. But I can honestly say, without Him, nothing else matters. With Him, He can make all things Matter!"

I was lost in thought and hadn't heard my neighbor approach and was startled by the clapping behind me. "I didn't know anyone else was listening," I said a bit embarrassed.

"I didn't want to interrupt you. I know the peonies loved it, and I'm certain your students will too. Don't change a word."

● ● ●

**Parent Prayer:** Lord, thank You for the lessons of maturity You've patiently taught me. Help me to pass these lessons on to the younger generation. Help me to earn the right to speak Your wisdom to Our children, so that they might seek You first.

**Seeds of Wisdom:** Find times to spend one-on-one time with each child. Set specific age marks—12, 16, 18 years old—and discuss the things they are about to be confronted with. Give them alternatives to peer-pressure, explain the hormone roller coaster, the exit strategies they need to develop. With our daughter, we enjoyed special teas, trips to a Shakespearean Festival and with our son; we skied and perused car shows. My husband took our daughter on dinner and movie dates, and he and our son were hunting buddies. We built memories and we were able to take the time to interject our values into their thinking at appropriate intervals.

**Garden Tip:** Old gardens have a beauty far beyond newer gardens because their gardeners have learned what blooms well in specific spots and what doesn't. An old garden has planted more of the best plants and discarded the weak plants. And a well-maintained garden draws visitors to it, where there might be an opportunity to share gardening tips!

You can find Pam's books on Amazon, at Barnes & Noble, garden stores, hospitals and on Pam's website www.PamalaJVincent.com

*Lessons From the Garden* is a series of 5 books:
> *Seeds of Daily Inspiration*
> *The Real Dirt on Being Happy*
> *Seeds of Wisdom for Parents*
> *For the Love of Pets*
> *Holidazes!*

**Other books by Pam**

*Learning Styles:*
> *Understanding the way you and your child learn*

*Getting the Job for Teens and College Bound Students:*
> *Techniques for Guaranteeing Your Success*

*Between a Rock and a Teenager:*
> *Unleashing Your Teen's Potential*

*Teen Exit Strategy Techniques:*
> *Earning Your Way Out with Respect*

*You Are More Than Enough:*
> *Define Yourself - Design Your Life*

Check out PamalaJVincent.com for her latest books, speaking engagements, YouTube videos and On Demand Class trainings.

www.ingramcontent.com/pod-product-compliance
Lightning Source LLC
Chambersburg PA
CBHW061220070526
44584CB00029B/3910